Canada and
CONFLICT

PATRICK JAMES

ISSUES IN CANADA

OXFORD
UNIVERSITY PRESS

OXFORD

UNIVERSITY PRESS

Oxford University Press is a department of the University of Oxford.
It furthers the University's objective of excellence in research, scholarship,
and education by publishing worldwide. Oxford is a registered trade mark
of Oxford University Press in the UK and in certain other countries.

Published in Canada by
Oxford University Press
8 Sampson Mews, Suite 204,
Don Mills, Ontario M3C 0H5 Canada

www.oupcanada.com

Library and Archives Canada Cataloguing in Publication
James, Patrick, 1957–
Canada and conflict / Patrick James.

(Issues in Canada)
Includes bibliographical references and index.
ISBN 978-0-19-543220-6

1. Canada—Foreign relations—21st century. 2. Canada—
Military policy. I. Title. II. Series: Issues in Canada

FC242.J34 2012   327.71   C2012-902401-5

To Klaus D. Ruttger

Printed and bound in the United States of America

1 2 3 4 – 15 14 13 12

Contents

List of Tables

Acknowledgements

During the summer of 2011, I had the good fortune to be an Eccles Professor of North American Studies for the British Library. I wrote the first draft of this book while in England. I appreciate very much the support of the British Association for American Studies, which made my time as an Eccles Professor possible. At the British Library I benefited from the superb advice of Philip Hatfield and Gerry Jenkins. The source material I located as a result of Gerry's mastery of government documents proved invaluable in particular. I also appreciate the efforts of Philip Davies from the British Library; he made arrangements and answered questions along the way that made my stay all the more enjoyable.

I am grateful to Michael Brecher, Carolyn C. James, Steve Saideman, and Ian Sirota for their insightful critiques of this work at the manuscript stage. Greg Anderson, Nic Choquette-Levy, and Chris Sands offered helpful ideas in setting boundaries for this study. Rahel Gebreyes provided a critique of the volume's introduction. Rahel Gebreyes, Evelyne Kim, and Somtochukwu Ugwueze, under the guidance of Indira Persad, provided valuable research assistance.

Chapter 1

Introduction

Overview

How does Canada relate to the world of conflict around it? For an advanced state with a history of more than 14 decades, security policy is a vast subject. The focus of this book will be on the most recent decade of Canadian experience, the one starting approximately with the new millennium. The traumatic day we have come to call 9/11 set in motion a range of new perceptions and policies around the world. That day will be the specific point of demarcation for this volume's treatment of Canada in conflict.

Some interesting issues regarding security policy can be mentioned only in passing, including climate change, the UN, the developing world, and other prominent matters with connections to national security. Instead, the issues included in this volume are those that focus *primarily* on security.[1] Clearly it is impossible to separate security from other issues in an all-or-nothing way. A decision about going to war, for example, clearly falls very close to one end of the security spectrum. Canadian refusal to join the US-led "Coalition of the Willing," which went to war against Iraq in 2003, is discussed below. Toward the other extreme would be the issue of whether to sign a treaty about the environment. An example in recent years would be the Copenhagen Accord (2009), from the UN Framework Convention on Climate Change, a non-binding extension of the Kyoto Protocol (1997). Its provisions call for upgraded emissions controls that might affect economic performance—and therefore military capability and security policy—in indirect ways.

This book addresses a set of interlocking questions:

- Is Canadian security policy different than before? If so, how?
- Do Canadians have an accurate sense of their place on the international stage?

- Is Canada performing well in terms of decision making, and in what ways can it do better?
- In what ways is Canada unique?
- What is Canada's likely future direction in security policy?

Security Issues

Assessing Canadian security policy begins with the national preoccupation of the last decade: the Afghan war. Afghanistan became Canada's first war in many decades. While virtually all observers agree that Canadian involvement in the war is significant, consensus ends there. Reactions to the Afghan war range from pride to scorn. The Canadian role in Afghanistan occupies a primary position in security policy over the last decade and thereby offers an opportunity to investigate a highly complex conflict.

An understanding of the situation in Afghanistan funnels out toward the topic of security relations with the United States (abbreviated to Can/Am)—through which so many issues are filtered. There are other security issues than Afghanistan that have occupied secondary but nevertheless important roles over the last decade. These matters range in the parties involved, from bilateral to multilateral, but I consider each in the context of Can/Am relations. At one extreme are the bilateral issues of the American border itself and Ballistic Missile Defence (BMD). Other issues, such as Canadian roles in the interventions in Iraq and Libya, contain significant multilateral elements. Still further along is Arctic sovereignty, which at least in principle is a matter of global concern and competition.

What, then, is the anticipated impact of the government and domestic politics on Canadian security policy? Canada from 9/11 onward so far includes governments led by three prime ministers: Jean Chrétien (Liberal, prior to 11 September 2001 to 12 December 2003), Paul Martin (Liberal, 12 December 2003 to 6 February 2006), and Stephen Harper (Conservative, 6 February 2006 to present). For these governments and their predecessors, security policy is influenced significantly by domestic politics, most notably by public opinion regarding the United States. Canada and the US share a border of 8,891 kilometres, or 5,525 miles. Economic interdependence for these countries, most directly visible in the cross-border exchange of people and products, is extraordinary. In the era following trade liberalization through the Canada–United States Free Trade Agreement and the North American Free Trade Agreement, the resulting degree of interconnectedness would rival any pair of states in the world.[2]

Bureaucratic politics matter in decision making as well, with Canada as no exception. "While assuring ministers that they share their objectives," one expert on the world of Ottawa observes, "officials will shape their policy advice in such a way as to achieve the preferred approach of the bureaucracy" (Hart 2008, 61). Moreover, this will also be true, albeit at a reduced level, for the domain of security policy.

Canada's basic challenge in security policy, therefore, is to manage its intricate relationship with the US (Doran 1984; Hart 2008, 334). This turns out to be an exercise in threading the needle. Ottawa needs to maintain good relations with Washington, but not to the extent that the prime minister appears to be in the back pocket of the president. Thus some middle ground needs to be occupied, but finding that middle ground is difficult from one issue to the next.

Summary of Chapters

Chapters 2 and 3 will reveal that much more is involved with Canada and Afghanistan than a simple treatment of the war's outbreak. Canadian participation went through multiple decision points and concerned both military security and development roles.

Chapter 2 sets the context and examines the causes of Canada's entry into the Afghan war, covering the historical background, along with the onset of the war. With regard to context, Canada and Afghanistan are a study in contrasts, with one state enjoying a long peace and the other ravaged by seemingly endless warfare. Canada's initial decision about joining the US and NATO in a war to overthrow the Taliban was caused by concerns ranging from security to trade and even national image.

Chapters 3 and 4 focus on the characteristics and consequences of Canada's war experience. As the conflict moved forward, the Canadian Force's (CF) location and role shifted dramatically upward into war-fighting in Kandahar. Reactions at home varied, to say the least. Consequences, at least in the short term, included an increased presence for the CF and a mindset that departed from the prior emphasis on human security. All things considered, Afghanistan emerges as a natural starting point for the study of Canada and conflict during the decade after 9/11.

Chapters 5 and 6, which focus on Can/Am relations, reflect a realistic sense of Canadian security policy as practised for a long time. Whether vilified or glorified, the US is recognized by all opinions as the filter through which world events are experienced in Canada.[3] This is a comment not so much on Canada itself as the agenda-setting role played by the world's lone superpower regarding security issues. As a neighbour to the US, Canada must deal with possible collateral effects from Washington's activity around the world on a daily basis. The US faces some challenges simply because it is the Rome of its day; and its supremacy has no serious rivals. Even likely suspects for the challenger role, such as China, currently lack the overall presence of the US around the globe.

Chapters 5 and 6 encompass a range of security issues for Canada in relation to the US. With origins before Confederation, border security is the most long-standing among the issues on the list. Arctic security becomes more prominent toward the end of the last century because of ongoing and anticipated effects from climate change. BMD moves in and out of prominence over several decades, with Ottawa perceiving significant time pressure for response about whether to participate a few years after 9/11 when the US eventually raised the matter in a very visible way. Canadian involvement in the Iraq War and Libyan intervention are issues arising in the last decade. Chapter 5 looks at the contexts of the preceding set of issues, along with the role of 9/11 as an activating cause for policy responses across the board. In Chapter 6, characteristics and consequences of the respective issues are reviewed.

Chapter 7 attempts to summarize Canada in relation to a world of conflict. In the new millennium, Canada had its first experience as a full-fledged military combatant in half a century. It continues to be involved with Afghanistan; economic aid and training of police and military personnel remain in place. After 9/11, Canada is living next door to a state that continues to lead the world, yet the US arguably does so in a state of aftershock, gradual recovery, and uncertainty about its direction. An ensemble of other issues, as noted already, have varied in their influence on Can/Am security relations in the years following 9/11: border management, Arctic sovereignty, BMD, Afghanistan, the War in Iraq, and intervention in Libya.

After reflecting on Afghanistan and other important security issues, this volume seeks to answer an overarching and multi-faceted question: Is Canada different than before as a result of its post-9/11 experiences regarding security policy and, if so, how? As it turns out, various perspectives on international relations will contribute to answering that question.

Chapter 2

A Country (Un)ready for War

How and Why?

How did Canada become involved in Afghanistan and do so in a way that continues to raise controversy over a decade later? Is the venture in Afghanistan about a sense of obligation Canada had to the US after 9/11, or is there more to it? What is the potential legacy of Canada's sustained role in the Afghan war? These and other related questions continue to stimulate interest among Canadians.

When updated histories of Canada are published, the war in Afghanistan is certain to receive its own detailed chapter. Interpretations, however, are likely to be far less predictable than the substantial amount of attention the subject will obtain. Both the content and impact of the Canadian role in Afghanistan are likely to be debated for many years to come.

This chapter and the two after it attempt to answer the questions of "how?" and "why?" regarding the Canadian years in Afghanistan. How did Canada, a country that for a long time rejected war, become involved in an intense military conflict that was taking place about as far away as possible without leaving the planet? Why did Canada go to Afghanistan and stay for so long, at least by national standards for involvement in combat? In response to these questions, Chapters 2, 3, and 4 explore the context, causes, characteristics, and consequences of the Canadian experience in Afghanistan. This answers the question of "how?" Perspectives based on realism, liberalism, the world of ideas, and the government and domestic politics are applied to explain the unfolding events in each chapter. This responds to the question of "why?" Given the scope of the subject matter, the present chapter focuses on context and causes, while Chapters 3 and 4 cover characteristics and consequences, respectively.

This chapter begins by exploring the context for the dramatic and destructive events of 9/11. Canada and Afghanistan are described along the dimensions most relevant to their later intense involvement with each other. Experiences with cooperation and conflict are natural priorities in setting each respective international context. A discussion of cause and effect comes next. How and why did Canada come to enter the US-led war against the Taliban in response to 9/11?

Context: (Un)ready for War

Canada and Afghanistan, the central actors in this drama, existed in very different international contexts prior to the transforming events of 11 September 2001. One of these countries, Canada, had enjoyed decades of relative tranquility. This sparsely populated but highly developed country sat next to the US superpower and had undergone no significant combat experience since the Korean War. (Exceptions such as Bosnia and bombing missions in Kosovo and Cyprus had not been sustained combat engagements.) The other country, Afghanistan, could not have been more different. It had endured decades of turmoil and war, both civil and interstate. Thus by background and circumstance, Afghanistan and Canada stood at opposite poles in terms of readiness for intense conflict.[1]

Prior to the last decade, which produced a major deployment to Afghanistan, Canada would seem to have been unlikely to carry out a significant military intervention on the other side of the world. With Lloyd Axworthy, Minister of Foreign Affairs, as the leading light, Canada downplayed any traditional role for the military throughout the 1990s. Axworthy led an initiative in favour of human security rather than foreign policy based on more traditional notions of national interest. The shift from state-oriented to human security produced an emphasis on working through international institutions, most notably UN peacekeeping. Canadians played a key role in advancing "responsibility to protect" as an official policy of the UN. Cooperation with transnational actors featuring a human security agenda became a staple of Canadian foreign policy. Canada, for example, led the way in producing an international treaty to ban the use of land mines.

Human security as a foreign policy orientation affected Canadian identity as well as policy. It produced among many Canadians a self-image of Canada as a *moral superpower* (Axworthy's term) in the making. As envisioned by advocates of a morally grounded foreign policy,

Canada would be at some distance from the US, with its capacity and interest in fighting wars. A limited military capability would be maintained, but only because peacekeeping demanded uniformed personnel with a minimal degree of training. At one point, Prime Minister Jean Chrétien even referred to peacekeeping as a Boy Scout type of activity (quoted in Shadwick 2006, 95).

Human security took hold to the point where it seemed, to many Canadians and especially those in younger age groups, to have always been the basis for thought and action regarding foreign policy. The growing popularity of this concept, operationalized in terms of peacekeeping, represented the logical outcome of a long-standing government trend away from a focus on national security. Given the reduced significance of that end, military capability could obviously be expected to diminish under the intense budgetary politics of Ottawa. The debacle in Somalia accelerated the downward trend for the CF.

Critics of the human security agenda expressed concern that Canadian foreign policy had moved in a direction that did not serve the national interest. They cited in particular the cumulative effect of a series of developments regarding the CF from the mid-1960s onward: "unification, budget cuts, personnel reductions, bilingualism, social engineering, and a failure to renew equipment gradually broke down morale and sapped professionalism" (Granatstein 2002, 422–23). These changes started with personnel; the CF lost 22,000 from its reserves and dozens of units closed around the country in 1965 (Blatchford 2008, 38–39).[2] Skeptics identified a wide range of problems that plagued the CF, not the least being military administrators. The CF had come to resemble a bureaucracy more than a fighting force at even a minimally acceptable level of readiness.[3] Actions by Canadian governments over previous decades, in sum, had reduced the Canadian military to peacekeeping as its overarching mission. Thus the 1990s represented a point of culmination for the CF's "downward slide" over three decades (Granatstein 2002, 420; see also Richter 2006, 51; Hillier 2010, 11; Welsh 2004, 23).

Consider military preparedness in particular. General Rick Hillier offers a sharply worded rebuke about that subject to Canadian governments from the years leading up to 9/11 (Hillier 2010). With a career spanning more than three decades, including the office of Chief of the Defence Staff (CDS), Hillier provides a personal account of the path to decrepitude from the 1970s onward. He points to a "distinct lack of leadership" and sums up the CF's evolution in the following manner: "The army and the rest of the Canadian Forces—after decades of training, few operations, a Cold War, government inattention and being on the back burner in Canada—were becoming a bureaucratic organization, just another department of the Government of Canada, administered by managers, not leaders" (Hillier 2010, 46–47, 158).

Hillier (2010, 109) leaves nothing to the imagination when providing examples of decision making that reduced capability and weakened readiness to act; he describes the sale of the heavy lift helicopters, the Chinooks, to the Netherlands as "one of the most idiotic decisions ever made in the Canadian Forces." This observation feeds into the general's more encompassing point, made by other critics as well, about diminishing mission capability versus rising demands made on the CF. During the 1990s, the government demanded that the CF function in what increasingly could be described as peacebuilding or peace enforcement operations, as opposed to purely peacekeeping. Difficult challenges such as Somalia and Bosnia, according to pro-military critics, "took the Canadian forces to, and in some cases past, the breaking point" (Hillier 2010, 115). The CF lacked both the personnel and equipment to conduct these new, much more challenging missions that transcended traditional peacekeeping.[4]

Upon taking office in 2003, Chrétien accelerated existing trends away from support for the CF. He immediately cancelled contracts for the replacement of obsolete Sea King and Labrador helicopters with EH-101 helicopters. This dramatic action—justified in terms of Ottawa's financial problems—included a $473 million cancellation fee (Richter 2006, 62). Chrétien, in his memoirs, puts forward his justification for limiting support to the CF (Chrétien 2008, 303):

> every government is under constant pressure to spend more and more on defence. . . . The Canadian Forces always claimed it needed more tanks and guns, more submarines and destroyers, more bombers and helicopters, but I wasn't always sure that its self-interest was the same as the national interest. During the period of high deficits and major cutbacks, it was hard as a matter of principle, politics, and the heart to buy new equipment for the military while reducing assistance to the poor, the ill, and the old.

The preceding account shows suspicion of the CF, which the prime minister links to the US government, as being at least somewhat politically motivated in the quest for resources. In short, Chrétien wonders aloud why anyone would expect further military spending without more pressing reasons, especially in an era of extreme retrenchment.

Public respect for the military reached its low point around the same time. A scandal over military conduct during the peacekeeping mission in Somalia had been sufficient to bring about the abolition of the Canadian Airborne Regiment—precisely the kind of force needed for light, rapid-strike capability (Pigott 2007, 86). This dismissal reflected the government's need to "do something" to placate a mass public that held its military in rather low esteem. A compelling study of public opinion explains Canada's lack of forceful reaction to the Rwandan genocide in 1994 with a comparison that seems incredible now: "Canadians had come to believe that the inherent racism of their own armed forces was worse than that in Rwandan society at large" (Kirton and Guebert 2007, 2). The mindset against the CF had strengthened to a level that can be described only as surreal, given the loss of more than 800,000 lives in Rwanda at the time. While other countries failed to show a forceful reaction to Rwanda, the stated Canadian priority on peacekeeping made Ottawa's inaction especially conspicuous.

Placement of the human security and peacekeeping concepts as centrepieces of Canadian foreign policy merely recognized a process already long underway—one that entailed at least an implicit commitment to avoid combat operations. "Our priorities," as described by Chrétien (2008, 304), "were international peacekeeping through the United Nations or NATO, defending the boundaries of North America and the citizens of Canada, and fighting terrorism at home and abroad, and we adjusted our spending to reflect those priorities." The prime minister, not surprisingly, claimed that his government had recognized that a new situation existed after 9/11; Ottawa, from his point of view, had reacted quickly and effectively with an allocation of $8 billion to security measures (Chrétien 2008, 304).

Leaders in the CF, with their more direct experience regarding deployments, tended to be less enthusiastic about what some referred to as the peacekeeping "mantra" or "bubble" in the pre-9/11 era (Hillier 2010, 153; see also Hart 2008, 90). The world had been changing in ways that challenged the typical sense of ideal peacekeeping that pervaded Canadian thinking. The standard idea of a peacekeeping deployment went something like this: Canadian military forces would interpose themselves after a conflict, keep the peace, and permit cooler heads to prevail.

What if, however, there is no peace to keep? This possible dilemma is more in line with the evolving but largely unnoticed shift in the nature of global instability during the 1990s. Missions such as Kosovo suggested that peacebuilding and even enforcement, as opposed to the safer non-combat role of peacekeeping, would be needed much more often in the post–Cold War era. (During one of those missions, the 2nd Battalion Princess Patricia's Canadian Light Infantry [PPCLI] at the Medak Pocket in Croatia may have been the first Canadian soldiers to experience combat since the end of the Korean War [Blatchford 2008, 73].) No longer could it be assumed that UN-sanctioned peacekeepers would keep apart (at least somewhat) obedient proxies of the US and USSR, with low degrees of risk regarding casualties and material damage. The "Pearsonian" model of peacekeeping, admired by Canadians during the Cold War, had become obsolete (Windsor, Charters, and Wilson 2008, 12–13; see also Canada 2006b, 57; Travers and Owen 2008, 702).[5] Instead, as in Kosovo, Canadian troops could expect to be in harm's way during future missions, with an expanding range of responsibilities related to nation building. UN efforts in Cambodia, Somalia, and Haiti had transitioned into such peace enforcement and peacebuilding (Canada 2006b, 58; see also Windsor, Charters, and Wilson 2008, 15).

Disorder in the post–Cold War world featured groups that seemed capable of extreme violence while also answering to no one. Events such as the Rwandan genocide in particular revealed that the UN as a Cold War institution simply could not meet the challenges it once did through conventional peacekeeping deployments, for example, as it had in Cyprus, within which Canadians had played a prominent role. The world after the collapse of the Soviet empire instead created challenges in unfamiliar places from entities that looked nothing like conventional nation-states and involved a range of issues that superseded capitalism versus communism or other straightforward dimensions. Transnational entities that engaged in what the West would label "terror tactics" came to the forefront, with radical Islam increasingly prominent beyond its historical base in the Middle East and Central Asia.

What, then, should Canada do when faced with such dangerous and unpredictable situations? What would be the rules of engagement for the CF when deployed? From the standpoint of words versus deeds, Canada on the eve of 9/11 existed in a state of latent contradiction. It supported the responsibility to protect as a concept, but what would this mean in practice? Canada had endorsed the concept of human rather than national security as the grounds for multilateral intervention under the auspices of the UN. However, therein lies the paradox. If faced with a "put up or shut up" situation, with *what* would Canada intervene? When the sun came up on 9/11, the CF had no effective air or sea lift. It also possessed reserves inadequate to sustain anything beyond a brief mission. Moreover, Canadians generally had come to see their military in a traditional peacekeeping role, so the gaps in capability just noted had not stirred much controversy as yet (with the exception of the huge penalty for cancellation of the above-noted helicopter contract).

All of this—an activist doctrine combined with limited military capability and near non-existent public support for the use of force—comes together to highlight a major point of irony: "the government and its people are turning the responsibility for defending Canada and its national interests over to the Americans" (Granatstein 2002, 427). Yet the rationale for human security, at least in part, had been to break *away* from the national security- and military-oriented foreign policy associated with the US. Canada would pursue a foreign policy based on moral considerations, with an emphasis on protecting people, as opposed to a traditional focus on national interests.

Canada's quest for an identity separate from the US had started much earlier and provided an ongoing justification for reducing the CF as a potential military instrument of foreign policy. The primary goal of the Third Option, proposed by Prime Minister Pierre Elliott Trudeau at the outset of the 1970s, was to move Canada away from its traditional focal points, in succession, of Britain and the US. In line with those who followed him in office (and regardless of their views about the US), Trudeau had been against the use of military force to achieve foreign policy goals. With time, and obviously without full awareness among leadership, the decline and fall of the CF put Canada in a position of greater dependence on the US with respect to any situation that might entail military combat capabilities. In other words, aversion to military *ends* caused the decay of *means*—namely, the CF—essential to any number of other purposes.

Canada, in words, identified with the cause of protecting people from oppression. In deeds, however, Canada could not match its lofty stated goals. The country had stared down a major budget crisis in the mid-1990s, and the military found no favour with those in power; as a result, the CF became a natural target for further reductions across the board (Goldenberg 2006, 189). With its emphasis on peacekeeping as carried out in recent decades, the Chrétien government in particular saw no rationale for maintaining combat readiness. It reduced the defence budget by 30 percent (Granatstein and Oliver 2011, 77; see also Canada 2006b, 58, 62–64; Richter 2006, 64; Kite and Nord 2007, 262). In fairness to the government of the day, and following on from the earlier quotation from the prime minister, what support would there be for protection of the military budget when even highly valued social programs had to be considered for spending cuts? Rhetoric thus became a cost-effective substitute for the capability to act in the realm of foreign policy.

Danger signals regarding weak capacity in comparison to potential challenges from abroad sounded toward the end of the millennium. In 1998 the Auditor General's report pointed to an approaching crisis in Canadian defence capability. The next year, Kosovo revealed equipment shortcomings sufficient to attract public attention (Richter 2006, 65).

No matter the issue—Afghanistan or another crisis, or before or after 9/11—Canada's position next to the US has always played a central role in setting its context. US leadership, especially on the military side, increasingly saw Canada as lacking in commitment as a result of its substantial reductions in defence spending during the 1990s. When it came to continental security and Canada, the US—to the extent that it thought about Canada at all—had negative perceptions. Canada increasingly appeared to be a "free rider" and, even in the eyes of Canadians taking a hard look at the situation, "to a significant degree that allegation was correct" (Stein and Lang 2007, 13; see also Hart 2008, 256).

Events on 9/11 brought the Canadian contradiction involving means and ends into bold relief. Faced with a potential deployment to Afghanistan, the CF had to meet a significant challenge in terms of available human and material resources. The most serious concerns included "training capacity, helicopter support, sea and air transport, and the protection of personnel from mines and improvised explosives [IEDs]" (Granatstein and Oliver 2011, 4–5). (Even the US, however, had problems with IEDs.) Add to that the sheer size of Afghanistan as the site for deployment—647,000 square kilometres, or about the size of Manitoba—and it is one of the few countries in the world with no railway system (Pigott 2007, 13, 35). Logistically speaking, this mission would dwarf Bosnia, which had proven to be quite a challenge to humanitarian intervention in its day. An accompanying degree of unfamiliarity is put colourfully in a description of Kabul, Afghanistan's principal city, proffered by an experienced traveller: "Even if you don't believe that Kabul was founded by the biblical Cain, son of Adam, the city was still said to be as exotic as Casablanca, as lawless as the Shanghai of the 1930s, and as far off the tourist trail as Lhasa before the package tours" (Pigott 2007, 12). Kabul, as would be agreed upon quite readily, is the *most* stable and predictable place in Afghanistan. The country as a whole virtually defies comprehension when it comes to the degree of mistrust, disorder, and violence that have characterized life there.

Afghanistan features a high level of suspicion regarding the outside world (Pigott 2007, 26). Landlocked and made up of difficult terrain, it is inaccessible and tends to be a natural incubator for such suspicion.[6] Such views become stronger with distance from the capital: "rural people have never wanted anything from Kabul except to be left alone" (Pigott 2007, 24). Significant areas of Afghanistan have never been under effective control by a central authority that provided any positive experience with government. Thus it becomes reasonable to ask whether Afghanistan lacks the minimal degree of integration essential to being designated as a sovereign state at all—a poor prospect for intervention of any kind.

Few entities, dating back to Alexander the Great, have such a long and accomplished history of resisting outside invasion. Whether the disaster that befell the British in the nineteenth century or the Soviets in the twentieth century, *failure* is the watchword of attempts by great powers to subdue Afghanistan. No theme comes up more in the research on this central Asian entity: Afghans successfully resisted "every foreign incursion and gained a fearsome reputation as tough, unbeatable guerrilla fighters" (Windsor, Charters, and Wilson 2008, 2; see also Smith 2007, 12). "No other country," observes Day (2010, 46; see also Pigott 2007, 18, 41), "boasts such a record of defeating imperial superpowers." In all instances the Afghans defeated more technologically advanced adversaries through sheer persistence. After so much fighting, Afghans are "inured to casualties in a way that Westerners are not" (Blatchford 2008, 255). When on the losing end of a battle, Afghans do not quit, even in the face of a great power adversary. Instead, they melt into the hills, with access to Pakistan in particular, in order to regroup and fight another day. This asymmetry in willingness to suffer, including casualties and material damage, would rear its head in a sustained way during Canadian deployment to Afghanistan.

Western- and Pakistan-backed guerrillas forced the Red Army and its puppet regime out of Afghanistan in 1989. Devastation occurred over the decade of struggle against the USSR, but it is important to remember that Afghanistan had started from a very low base in terms of development anyway. Outside of just a few cities, Afghanistan consisted of "low mud-brick buildings with flat roofs" and its people never have had access to running water or electricity (Stein and Lang 2007, xiv).

Victory over the USSR came at great cost; it made a shambles of Afghanistan both physically and possibly even as the idea of a country. This intense conflict, which evicted a regime imposed by the USSR, destroyed even the limited infrastructure that did exist. The war killed, wounded, or starved more than a million people and drove one-third of the population into exile (Windsor, Charters, and Wilson 2008, 5–6). One estimate from the UN asserted that it would take approximately 500 years to clear Afghanistan of the mines that had accumulated there (Pigott 2007, 13). A pessimist might guess that a very long time, if not centuries, also would be needed for the consciousness of the Afghan people to recover from the combination of traumatic experiences that had accumulated within living memory.

Fragmentation of the Afghan state as an idea accompanied the staggering material damage. As a result of so many long-lasting conflicts, Afghanistan had become "a multi-ethnic society, with loyalties defined largely by local ethnicity and geography, which limited the authority of any central Afghan government over its subjects" (Windsor, Charters, and Wilson 2008, 2–3). Tajiks in the north and Pashtuns in the south eyed each other with great uncertainty as the Soviet-backed regime collapsed.

Warlords who drove out the Soviets competed for control in various localities, guaranteeing that insecurity would continue to be the norm.

Associated with the legacy of fighting is the lack of Western assistance to the Afghanistan that came out of the ashes of Soviet occupation (Pigott 2007, 44; Independent Panel 2008, 20).[7] (This story is told with some degree of artistic licence in the Hollywood movie *Charlie Wilson's War*.) Without support to build infrastructure and provide stability, Afghanistan quickly descended into civil war among the factions that had thrown out the Soviets. The Soviet Union's ideology, which featured an atheistic, communist world view, played into the hands of resistance mobilized on the basis of religious beliefs, even those that might seem heinous in their own way. The long fight with the USSR opened the door for Islamists of whatever stripe to put themselves forward as a "made in Afghanistan" alternative.

Would-be Soviet domination had been replaced by no rule at all. "By 1994," observes Pigott (2007, 49), "even the pretense of a centralized government in Kabul had disappeared, and bandits and private armies of warlords roamed the country." The UN estimated that 25,000 civilians died in that year because of rocket and artillery attacks against Kabul alone (Pigott 2007, 46). Ominously, the Taliban gained control over multiple provinces in the south during 1994 and built momentum as a serious contender for power at the national level.

After so much violence, Afghans wanted order above all else. This explains an otherwise puzzling ascent to power for another dictatorship, that of the Taliban. The Taliban won the latest phase of the Afghan civil war by providing a coherent and organized alternative under conditions of chaos (Sinno 2010). Only a fragment of the country in the north remained out of the Taliban's control after their victory in September 1996. Warlords in that region, known as the United Islamic Front (or, in the West, the Northern Alliance), waited for an opportunity to challenge the Taliban's rule but offered no coherent option for governance.

Inspired by religious fanaticism, the Taliban practised a warped version of Islam that brought to mind the Dark Ages. Once in power, they forced women out of public life. Even worse, women lost access to education and medical care (Pigott 2007, 53). The radical interpretation of the Quran favoured by the Taliban ran to the bizarre: kite flying, long favoured by Afghans, became illegal. In March 2001, world attention became fixed on Afghanistan when the government destroyed the Buddhas of Bamiyan, monumental statues carved into the walls of a valley that had been standing for more than 1,400 years. While the UN urged the Taliban not to destroy this UNESCO World Heritage Site, they went ahead regardless, foreshadowing an even more violent action to come.

Dictatorship inflicted by the Taliban on the Afghan people amounted to nothing less than totalitarianism, backed up by a willingness to crush any opposition. The regime, therefore, did manage to create a "general sense of security" (Day 2010, 137; see also Pigott 2007, 50). This feeling of safety had been absent for a long time and therefore possessed great appeal, but in practice, rule by the Taliban meant only an end to the immediate threat of fatalities through civil war. Support for the Taliban, therefore, reflected not their brand of Islam but their "capacity to police the streets" (Stein and Lang 2007, 30–31).

Even with time and experience, the Taliban proved "both incapable of and unwilling to manage the economy or food production and distribution" (Windsor, Charters, and Wilson 2008, 9). By 1999, the Taliban permitted opium to be cultivated because of its profitability and the fact that Westerners (i.e., infidels) consumed it (Pigott 2007, 56). Farmers quickly came to depend on the high revenue from poppy sales, which overshadowed anything that could be made from legitimate agriculture.

From the standpoint of foreign policy, the Taliban's support for al Qaeda (i.e., "The Base") emerged as its most important trait. Osama bin Laden's assault against the US on 9/11 could be traced directly to the Taliban's sponsorship of al Qaeda. Devastation of the World Trade Center and damage to the Pentagon, along with a plane crash in rural Pennsylvania, set the stage for a US-led invasion and an expanding role for Canada in Afghanistan over the subsequent decade.

The geostrategic setting is essential to understanding the context of the Afghan war. Most significant is the long-standing and, from the standpoint of Canada and its allies, pernicious role played by Pakistan. The ethnic makeup of Afghanistan and Pakistan comes to the forefront here. Pakistan's border areas serve as home to 28 million Pashtuns, while 15 million of this same ethnic group live in Afghanistan (Stein and Lang 2007, 26–27). The border between these countries, a legacy of the British colonial era, is known as the Durand Line. It remains mostly unmarked and highly disputed (Smith 2007, 13). The dispersed Pashtuns moved back and forth virtually at will, each country blames the other for giving aid and comfort to its respective criminals and enemies (Windsor, Charters, and Wilson 2008, 155). Thus Pakistan pursues both geostrategic and ethnic agendas in the ongoing struggle for Afghanistan.

Devastation caused by war with the Soviets, along with US reliance on Islamabad to deliver war *matériel*, turned Pakistan into an effective "power broker" in Afghanistan and helps to explain the Taliban's rise to power (Windsor, Charters, and Wilson 2008, 5–6). After the Soviet-sponsored regime fell from power, Pakistan backed the "best bet" in the Pashtun south, namely, the Taliban. Pakistan's support for Islamic

militants also fits in with greater interests in the region; this neighbour-
ing country "long regarded Afghanistan as its 'backyard'—territory that
provides Pakistan with the 'strategic depth' it otherwise lacks" (Windsor,
Charters, and Wilson 2008, 4). Pakistan hoped, in particular, to limit
Indian influence in Afghanistan (Pigott 2007, 199; Smith 2007, 5). This
intent did not diminish when the Afghan government sponsored al
Qaeda's assault on a putative ally, the US, on 9/11.

Afghanistan and Canada, obviously, had very different backgrounds
coming into the transforming events of 2001. Canada existed in a context defined by liberal thinking. Canadians, by and large, associated the
foreign policy of their country with the pursuit of human rather than
national security. Canada put these liberal goals into operational form
via multilateral initiatives, with special emphasis on UN-sponsored
peacekeeping. Thus Canadian foreign policy rejected a realist point of
view that would rely on the use of force in pursuit of national security.
Canada could act in this way because its geostrategic position entailed
a high degree of safety as a border state and principal ally of the US,
the world's only superpower. The government and domestic politics in
Canada featured a strong consensus against involvement in combat and
ongoing concerns about US unilateralism. From a realist point of view,
however, pre-9/11 Canada existed in an increasingly dangerous world
and was not well-prepared for the trials of likely future events.

Afghans lived in a world that might be viewed as realism gone mad—
close, perhaps, to the dystopia of a "war of all against all" as envisioned
by Thomas Hobbes centuries earlier against the backdrop of civil war in
England. Liberal notions of cooperation had no standing in a domain
where outside intervention always had meant intended domination
and thus the need to resist. Afghanistan under any regime also had to
cope with Pakistan, a meddlesome and even hostile neighbour since its
independence in 1947. In terms of government and domestic politics,
Afghans could not count on even the most basic services from their state,
which tended to exist more on paper than in practice beyond the local
level. Afghans, in sum, could not have been more opposite to Canadians
in prior experience as their encounter with each other approached.

Causes: 9/11 and Canada at War

Canada's role in 9/11 began immediately and entailed both loss of human
life and people's reaction to events as they unfolded on that fateful day.[8]
The attacks by al Qaeda on 9/11 killed 24 Canadians (Granatstein and
Oliver 2011, 4). In a touch of irony, US officials—usually near-oblivious
to their northern neighbour—reacted with shock and dismay when they

learned that a Canadian, Lieutenant General Finlay, was responsible through North American Aerospace Defence Command (NORAD) for air defence on the day of the attack (Fergusson 2010, 236). Their surprise reveals both the degree of integration that existed already in security and the asymmetry regarding the awareness of that integration on opposite sides of the border.

Canada dispatched hundreds of firefighters and emergency workers to Washington, DC, and New York City; Canadian air traffic controllers diverted more than 250 airplanes from US airports (Welsh 2004, 11). The CF provided relief to 23,921 passengers aboard the 142 civilian flights that had been diverted to six airports in Canada (Pigott 2007, 214). In the words of Chrétien (2008, 295), Canadians "did their country honour by opening their homes, their hearts, and their wallets to strangers in distress."

Canadians overwhelmingly condemned the attacks. They held vigils across the country (Lennox 2009, 91). Three days after 9/11, the prime minister, Governor General, and other officials participated in a massive rally on Parliament Hill to show solidarity with the US (Goldenberg 2006, 261; Chrétien 2008, 296). Some tensions did emerge when Bush failed to mention Canada in a list of those he thanked in a speech on September 20, but Chrétien quickly defused the situation (Chrétien 2008, 299–300).

Compelling evidence established the Taliban as sponsors of al Qaeda. The Canadian government "issued a blank-cheque offer of its military forces to the United States and became one of the first allies to send forces to Afghanistan" (Fergusson 2010, 215). Ottawa quickly decided to support US-led military action to overthrow Afghanistan's Taliban government, which ultimately took the form of Operation Enduring Freedom (OEF). Canada supported OEF through Operation Apollo.[9] Minister of Defence Art Eggleton began public deployment on September 20 by authorizing CF members on military exchange programs to participate in operations responding to 9/11. Various units in the CF began to receive warning orders about possible deployment to Afghanistan.

Washington, in two communications on September 20 and 21, demanded that the Afghan government turn over al Qaeda members (most notably Osama bin Laden) and close down terrorist training camps. The Taliban refused what amounted to an ultimatum, which made war with the US inevitable. The UN Security Council passed Resolution 1368 and the UN invoked Chapter VIII of its Charter, which authorized military force, on September 28 (Horn 2010, 13, 16).

Chrétien announced support for OEF, which involved both the US and UK, on October 7, the day it started. The Canadian effort would include all branches of the CF and began with a covert deployment. Canada's Joint Task Force 2, an elite military unit charged with carrying out special operations, had secretly entered Afghanistan by early December 2001 (Stein and Lang 2007, 11). The shock of 9/11 had produced high approval among Canadians (73 percent) for joining the US and declaring war against terrorism. Air strikes against the Taliban toward the end of 2001 also enjoyed support in Canada (Kirton and Guebert 2007, 14).

Canada's response took a multilateral form as well. NATO invoked Article 5 for the first time ever, with 9/11 being regarded as an attack on one member and thus an assault on the alliance as a whole that would justify a military response. Chrétien, in fact, went on the record before any other leader in calling for Article 5 to be invoked (Goldenberg 2006, 263).[10]

While it had been formidable against rival factions in the struggle to rule Afghanistan (Sinno 2010), the Taliban could not stand up to an invasion led by the US. The attack commenced on 7 October 2001 at 12:30 Eastern Standard Time (Pigott 2007, 64). Soon after, OEF drove the Taliban from power. On November 12 and 13, the Northern Alliance, which coordinated its actions with the US, liberated Kabul (Pigott 2007, 65). Osama bin Laden escaped from the Tora Bora mountains, probably into tribal regions via the White Mountain range (Lennox 2009, 93).

Canada played a necessarily limited role, under the auspices of Operation Apollo, during this initial and conventional phase of fighting. A Canadian task force played a supporting role in the Arabian Sea (Lennox 2009, 94). The CF, however, lacked strategic airlift and had to wear "heavy green-black-and-brown uniforms better suited to the forests of the Canadian shield" (Richter 2006, 66). By November 2001 the CF had available less than 15,000 reservists (Granatstein 2002, 423). This guaranteed considerable strain on the CF if required to maintain a presence abroad—especially one with a significantly larger number of troops—for any length of time. On the horizon loomed the challenges of security and stabilization for a territory that barely qualified as a country at all. Could a new Afghanistan be built out of the ashes of the old? In spite of its limited military resources at the time of the war's outbreak, Canada would come to play a major part in the answer to that question.

Why, then, did Canada respond so positively to the US call to arms? Perhaps the most obvious answer comes from realism: countering the threat to peace and security posed by al Qaeda's terrorist attacks required the use of military force (Independent Panel 2008, 20; Windsor, Charters, and Wilson 2008, 10). As a realist would expect, Canada pursued military means in response to a direct attack on its most important ally. This basic power-oriented story will be expanded to include other perspectives that sometimes work in combination with each other (and realism) to identify additional factors of importance.

Other elements of realism, along with aspects from the outlook based on government and domestic politics, can be combined to explain Canada's decision to go to war. With the US by far Canada's largest trading partner, the Canadian agenda from 9/11 onward focused on keeping the border open (Stein and Lang 2007, 6; see also Clarkson 2002, 401; Dey 2011, 2). (The US did close the border briefly; details are provided in Chapter 5.) Canada could not stay out of things but instead would have to become involved in some way to preserve its interests. Thus Canada "bandwagoned with a stronger state—the United States—because the cost of opposing the stronger power—the potential of a closed border—exceeded the benefits" (Dey 2011, 2; see also Welsh 2004, 15). Canadian leaders hoped to gain from supporting the US on Afghanistan while simultaneously reducing or even eliminating the risk of being among those countries that would end up paying a price for American anger after 9/11. "The prevailing emotion in Canada, in every department and organization, after September 11," observed Hillier (2010, 24), "was to try to get back to September 10. But that was just not possible." Thus the Chrétien government would have to make the best of things under difficult, highly constrained circumstances.

US concerns about border security constituted a real risk for Canada; even years after 9/11, American politicians continued to assert (falsely) that the 9/11 hijackers had some Canadian connection or even came across the Canada–US border. Thus the perceived need to join in with the Afghanistan war effort also can be traced to domestic politics in Canada. The government could expect significant constituencies to be outraged by economic losses that would follow from even a brief closure of the border (Dey 2011, 2–3).[11]

Realist and idea-based interpretations of Canada's entry into war combine to emphasize action based on power status. The decision to fight reflected a belief in "full engagement in international affairs in a manner befitting Canada's status as a member of the G8" (Sjolander 2009, 83). Anything less would weaken Canada as a leading country both as an idea and a material presence. Another element of this type of thinking concerns the reputation of the CF. The military response to 9/11 by Canada would counter criticism of the Canadian military at both home and abroad (Welsh 2004, 15). Greatly reduced or even gone would be accusations of free riding, especially in comparison to US efforts.

International norms, from an idea-oriented point of view, also drove Ottawa toward war (Dey 2011, 71). The attacks on 9/11 had been interpreted by Canada's allies not as a strike by the weak against the strong, nor, perhaps, as an isolated event, but instead as a throwing down of the gauntlet by radical Islamists against the free nations of the world. As articulated by President George W. Bush, the US would embark on a Global War on Terror (GWOT) in response to the violence perpetrated by al Qaeda. This type of war designated national rather than human security as a priority. A search for the underlying causes of 9/11 that might have been found in underdevelopment and anger about US influence around the globe, most notably as it came to threaten traditional and especially religiously inspired ways of life, would have been the alternative path. This human security–oriented option attracted no influential advocates among Canada's peers. The discourse of national security triumphed over human security in a fast-moving environment in which more subtle thinking had become very unlikely to find a positive reception in the aftermath of the intense violence on 9/11.

Whither Canada under such conditions? Ottawa bought into the new line from Washington, that is, the idea of a GWOT in response to radical Islam. From a realist point of view, this decision made perfect sense because threats had translated into highly damaging actions. Radical Islamists *did* constitute a danger to both human and national security. Without national security there could be no human security anyway, so Canada simply acted prudently in its perceived interests. At the same time, as per an account based on the government and domestic politics, Canada got more than it bargained for. Consider General Hillier's (2010, 244) observations on Operation Apollo, the initial stage of deployment to Afghanistan: "The government had so little understanding of things military that I don't believe it truly comprehended the mission to which it had just committed our soldiers, our first combat mission since the Korean War." As will become apparent in Chapter 3, neither the Canadian government nor society understood the full implications of an initial decision to support the US invasion of Afghanistan.

Idea-related factors can help to account for the rapid response from Canada in going to war. Quick movement by Ottawa in the obviously challenging and stressful policy environment created by 9/11 became easier because of (1) a "green light" from international institutions and (2) the presence of at least a superficial connection between the war option and established Canadian values.

First, NATO and the UN had endorsed the use of force as a response to the assault experienced by the US on 9/11 (Independent Panel 2008, 21). This meant that going to war would be in line with the norm of multilateral action under the rubric of international institutions. "As members of NATO, which is after all a self-defence pact," observed former prime minister Paul Martin (2008, 391), "we had a moral if not legal duty to support them. We also had self-interest in doing so." This multilateral venture served Canadian interests in another way as well: constraining an otherwise unilateral US. Canada clearly would have more leverage in a multilateral setting than otherwise. Thus Canada taking the leadership of the International Security Assistance Force (ISAF) in 2004 and going into Kandahar a year later both helped to put the war effort under the NATO, as opposed to US, rubric.

Second, values related to human security also play a role in explaining why Canada joined the US-led war so rapidly. As described by the Independent Panel (2008, 21, 22), which had the task of assessing further involvement in Afghanistan a few years later, a "fortunately endowed" state such as Canada "owed obligations to the international community" and therefore should engage in "promotion and protection of human security in fragile states." Afghanistan clearly fit the bill. This helps to explain both the Canadian entry into the war and its later persistence in the face of rising human and material costs. Of course, a realist might observe that the result is overdetermined: the emphasis on norms and ideas might simply stand as a rationalization for a decision that had been made primarily on the grounds of national interest.

The Story So Far

Leading up to their sustained encounter from 9/11 onward, Canada and Afghanistan existed in polar opposite contexts. Canada pursued a foreign policy based on human security, with action through international institutions and peacekeeping at the centre of things. As a long-standing democracy, Canada embodied liberal values and rejected the realist emphasis on national security and the possible use of military force to advance national interest. Afghanistan, by contrast, had no national government to speak of and lived in a setting of hyperrealism. Its people adopted a war-fighting posture out of necessity and had well-justified suspicions toward outsiders rather than a Canadian-style disposition to trust in international institutions.

Canada's entry into the war against Afghanistan, while unlikely given the context of each country, began most directly because of 9/11. The cause and effect evaluation starts out with a straightforward realist assessment in favour of answering an attack on one's ally with force, but other points of view combine with each other and elements of realism to provide a more complete explanation. Canada went to war because of material interests, such as keeping open its border with the US, and thereby acted in line with realist principles and concerns about domestic politics. Canada, from realist and idea-based standpoints, also acted to preserve its status as a leading country. Joining the US-led war effort complemented Canada's identity as a member of the Western elite. Finally, norms in favour of supporting allies through military means, along with the blessing of international institutions, added to the already significant reasons in favour of going to war. The next chapter will consider the characteristics of Canada's involvement in Afghanistan.

Chapter 3

The Afghan War: Battles at Home and Abroad

How and Why?

This chapter also considers the "how" and "why" regarding Canada in Afghanistan. The confirmed end of a Canadian combat role in 2011 allows for the short- and long-term effects of the mission to now be assessed.

Characteristics: In, Out, and Back In Again

Canada had joined the short and successful war led by the US against the Taliban, but that constituted, as Sir Winston Churchill might have put it, not the "beginning of the end" but the "end of the beginning." An initial military victory came quite easily in the late fall of 2001. However, some kind of government, along with significant reconstruction, would be needed to replace the Taliban (Stein and Lang 2007, 33–34; Windsor, Charters, and Wilson 2008, 11). Moreover, that work would need to take place in what remained an inhospitable location and therefore entail conventional combat, over and above providing purely reactive security for reconstruction. Afghanistan had known only fragmentation and various forms of dysfunctional would-be dictatorships in modern times. It rapidly became obvious that any new government with democratic principles would face an insurgency made up of those on the losing end of the conventional round of fighting just concluded. Thus Canada could expect a range of decision points concerning involvement. To what degree would it provide security, nation building, or both?

Multilateral efforts toward rebuilding Afghanistan started up as soon as the Taliban went down. Organized by the UN, a meeting of 35 prominent Afghans took place in Bonn, Germany, on 27 November 2001. This produced the Agreement on Provisional Arrangements in

Afghanistan Pending the Re-establishment of Permanent Government Institutions (Bonn Agreement) (Holland 2010, 277; Pigott 2007, 68). The Bonn Agreement called for an interim authority in Afghanistan to start the process of building a government (Horn 2010, 19). Under the control of NATO, the ISAF also came into being as a product of the Bonn Agreement (Holland 2009, 78). (UN Security Council Resolution 1386 had authorized ISAF on 20 December 2001.) Thus the Bonn Agreement began the process of putting together some kind of infrastructure for Afghanistan, with both political and military dimensions. The Loya Jirga, a grand council in the Afghan tradition that would correspond to a parliament understood in Western terms, approved the proposed constitution in December 2001.

Pragmatic in nature, the new constitution proclaimed Afghanistan an Islamic republic. On 22 December 2001, a 30-member governing committee, the Afghan Interim Authority (AIA), began work on nation building with the swearing in of Hamid Karzai as its head. Canada re-established diplomatic ties with the new Afghan state on 25 January 2002 (Pigott 2007, 88). Christopher Alexander, Canada's first ambassador to Afghanistan, took up his appointment on 3 July 2003 (Pigott 2007, 96). From a Canadian standpoint, this connection had an important purpose vis-à-vis encouraging further involvement with Afghanistan. The new regime had the ability to invite other governments to assist in nation building; Canadians, therefore, would not have to see themselves as interlopers.

Furthermore, the Bonn Agreement emphasized the development of Afghanistan through a specific operational means: Provincial Reconstruction Teams (PRTs). The AIA and its allies intended the multifaceted PRTs to have an impact on "governance and justice, security and stability, and development" (Pigott 2007, 139; see also Murray 2011, 155; Windsor, Charters, and Wilson 2008, 43). These teams, which usually included up to one hundred or so members (and sometimes significantly more), tailored their efforts to the region at hand: "In one province, the focus might be on supporting local government administration, in another it might be on training police, and in a third it might concentrate on infrastructure development" (Stein and Lang 2007, 97–98). Each PRT included a high-ranking military officer in command. A range of expertise would be needed, so civilians and military personnel worked side by side.[1]

From the outset, however, PRTs operated with some intrinsic flaws. As noted in the *Afghanistan Study Group Report* (CSPC 2008, 22), even years later, PRTs had "no overarching concept of operations or organizational structure" and individually lacked a unified chain of command.

Numerous factors, ranging from personalities and local politics to the funding and capability of the lead nation, caused priorities and performance to be quite uneven from one PRT to the next (CSPC 2008, 22; see also Maley 2008, 17).

Conditions for an insurgency with national scope ripened quickly in spite of efforts by the AIA and its partners from abroad to engage in reconstruction and development. Afghanistan could be described at any time as "a place so ethnically and culturally riven that it seems to be a country made for civil war" (Day 2010, 13). The observation became especially true of the situation that existed in a once again occupied Afghanistan. Consider the range of challenges identified by Day (2010, 48):

> In order for NATO to succeed in Afghanistan, a whole generation of warlords and fighters need to be divested of their interests, centuries-old ethnic divisions need to be mended, a country consisting mainly of semi-destroyed mud huts needs to be rebuilt, and it needs to be proven to every member of a population accustomed to violence and coercion that our way, democratic capitalism, is really their best option.

This summary draws attention to the diverse nature of the insurgency from the outset. It was not only the Taliban who confounded efforts to prevent Afghanistan from spiralling downward into a failed state. Disgruntled warlords, drug smugglers, and Islamic militants from outside the country also had incentives to preserve the existing state of disorder (Day 2010, 140). The adversary, from the standpoint of an outside intervention seeking stabilization, "is not so much an enemy as an attitude" (Pigott 2007, 170). Thus the post-2001 Afghan insurgency contrasts with the Viet Cong and other historical instances of unified, self-designated national liberation movements (Windsor, Charters, and Wilson 2008, 24; see also Pigott 2007, 169). Rather than fighting for any one cause in particular, the insurgents collectively opposed the latest occupation.

With limited numbers and firepower, the insurgency quickly adopted tactics intended to undermine the Afghan population's support for the new regime and its coalition of sponsoring governments. The Taliban began to leave threatening messages, known as *shabnamah* (night letters), in mosques and other locations and returned to villages after ISAF patrols left as an ongoing intimidation tactic (Windsor, Charters, and Wilson 2008, 24, 51). The struggle for allegiance at a local level got underway quickly and continues to this day.

Encounters with the insurgency produced a classification of its participants in terms of identity and associated fighting quality. Designated as Tier 1, hard-core fighters from the Taliban included many foreigners, such as Chechens, Saudis, and Pakistanis. By contrast, those described as Tier 2 lacked the same commitment and included "local Taliban and drug-trafficker militias" (Windsor, Charters, and Wilson 2008, 87). The existence of Tier 2 fighters opened a window of opportunity for the Canadians and their allies. If development efforts could yield results quickly enough, Tier 2 fighters might switch over to more constructive employment. This could weaken the insurgency in both material and psychological terms.

What about Afghan government capabilities? The answers here will have implications for the characteristics of Canadian involvement as it evolved over the decade. On paper, Afghanistan continued to make strides forward in terms of creating what could be recognized as a government; on 13 June 2002, the Loya Jirga elected Karzai as interim head of the Afghan Transitional Authority through the end of 2004. However, in light of the observations made in Chapter 2 about weak or even non-existent infrastructure, it is not surprising to learn that neither the Afghan National Army (ANA) nor the Afghan National Police (ANP) began with even a basic capability to stand up to the insurgency. Even years after multiple military forces from ISAF had worked with these organizations toward improved performance, ANA units continued to suffer from "corruption, drug abuse, ethnic rivalry and poor leadership," with the ANP receiving even worse criticism across the board (Chaudhuri and Farrell 2011, 274, 278; see also Stein and Lang 2007, 221–22; Blatchford 2008, 4–5; Wattie 2008, 168).

Shortcomings of the ANP and ANA added to a long list of other problems facing the intervening powers as they sized up their new ally: governance, infrastructure, ethnic divisions, tribalism, al Qaeda, difficult terrain, and opium (Day 2010,11). Afghanistan's situation contrasted starkly with, for instance, Western Europe in the rebuilding era of the Marshall Plan after World War II. Countries targeted for the ultimately successful assistance program in postwar Europe previously had been quite developed and recovered quickly. Development, like security, would begin from a near non-existent foundation in the case of Afghanistan.

Early reconstruction efforts outside of Kabul took place in a minimal way. In places such as Kandahar, well away from the capital, the Taliban targeted UN personnel and other aid workers and took advantage right away of their ability, when needed, to fade back into a local village (Windsor, Charters, and Wilson 2008, 21, 22, 23). With relatively limited deployments of their own, ISAF had difficulty dealing with these tactics. In the troublesome southern sector of Afghanistan, NATO (to be precise, this refers initially to ISAF) had just six soldiers per 100 square kilometres; this compared with 11 for Bosnia and 24 for Haiti (Smith 2007, 19). (These numbers changed significantly only with the US troop surge of 2010.) With security and reconstruction interdependent, the ability of insurgents to behave like chameleons, coupled with a limited capacity for labour-intensive efforts to establish their whereabouts, served as an ongoing obstacle to progress across the board.

Canada deployed the 3 PPCLI Battle Group to Kandahar in February 2002. This unit would work in tandem with the US on military operations. The deployment followed as an almost obvious consequence of sending Canadian soldiers under US command in the preceding November. Over a six-month tour of duty, the Battle Group's responsibilities included both security and combat.

Canadians began a ground offensive, conducted with the Americans, on 10 March 2002. Efforts to locate and neutralize Taliban fighters took the CF and their US allies into the Paktia Province. This mission encountered resistance and Canadian troops engaged with the enemy. In addition to Operation Anaconda during March, Canada participated in Operation Harpoon that same month. Other missions, in the Tora Bora region and Zabol Province, included reconnaissance and the destruction of cave complexes to which the Taliban might return.

Canada experienced a natural but unpleasant by-product of involvement in direct military action on 18 April 2002: a friendly fire incident. A US F-16 fighter jet killed four Canadian soldiers from the 3 PPCLI during a training mission (Pigott 2007, 90–91; Stein and Lang 2007, 19; Blatchford 2008, 43). The incident proved traumatic for a Canadian public unused to casualties and quite unfamiliar with the accidents that can and do happen with live ordnance and (especially) multiple military organizations attempting to work with each other. This accident also fed into Canadian stereotypes of Americans—and especially their military—being trigger happy. It is impossible to say what role the incident played specifically in Canadian decision making, but obviously it did not encourage further pursuit of a military role.

Ottawa decided to come home from Kandahar on 21 May 2002: "Defence Minister Art Eggleton announced that Canada would be pulling its ground presence out of Afghanistan by the end of July, leaving marine and air force personnel, as well as members of its Joint Task Force 2 in the conflict zone" (Sjolander 2009, 84). The 3 PPCLI Battle Group returned to Canada without replacement in July. This short-term reversal of the trend toward more engagement probably resulted from a combination of casualties and a lack of replacement soldiers (Kirton and Guebert 2007, 8). Canada had no "policy or plan" for Afghanistan beyond the summer of 2002 (Stein and Lang 2007, 20). Thus it assumed, by default, a reactive position vis-à-vis the US in particular. As with so many other previous conflicts, the US can and would be expected to take the lead as military engagements came to the forefront.

September 2002 brought important news from the US. The Minister of National Defence, John McCallum, learned that the US wanted the CF back in Afghanistan, with Kandahar as the deployment (Stein and Lang 2007, 43). General Hillier, a rising figure in the Canadian military, advocated this choice because of several perceived advantages: maximum international visibility; command of NATO south and battle group in Kandahar; the position of Kandahar as a linchpin for ISAF's success; the presence of Kandahar Air Field; proximity to major US combat units; the ability of the UK, Netherlands, and US to share expenses; improved relations with the US; and a combat role and grounds for modernizing the CF (Holland 2010, 279–80).

Requests for assistance from Washington coincided with a decline in Canadian support for the Afghan war as the US confrontation with Iraq heated up (Kirton and Guebert 2007, 16). While covered at greater length in Chapter 5 on US-Canada relations, a few points regarding the Iraq War are essential here. Chrétien expressed ongoing skepticism about the likelihood of an attack by Iraq with Weapons of Mass Destruction (WMDs) against the US. Moreover, the US planned to invade Iraq in league with a coalition of governments outside of a mandate from either the UN or NATO. Thus Afghanistan looked increasingly good in comparison if Canada felt the need to play some visible role in the unfolding GWOT led by the US. Al Qaeda terrorists sponsored by the Taliban had attacked the US, so its military response in Afghanistan had legitimacy under mandates from the UN and NATO.

Defence Minister John McCallum met in Washington, DC, with Secretary of Defence Donald Rumsfeld and others on 8 January 2003. It surprised McCallum to learn that, rather than serving in Kandahar, Rumsfeld wanted Canada in Kabul to lead ISAF. Remarks during the meeting conveyed Rumsfeld's mistaken belief that Afghanistan had moved past a purely military stage and would begin shifting soon into stabilization, development, and rebuilding (Stein and Lang 2007, 46–51). As would become obvious, the Afghanistan envisioned in the Bonn Agreement existed only as an ideal, and insurgents had yet to mount their most intense attacks on the fledgling regime and its allies.

Interesting to ponder, in light of earlier observations by General Hillier and others about the CF's state of readiness, is the military leadership's reaction to the proposed ISAF mission. Canadian officers generally regarded ISAF as "too dangerous, with no obvious end point or way to measure success" and lacking in rules of engagement (Stein and Lang

2007, 41). This observation refers back to the points from Chapter 2 regarding capability—or lack thereof—along with the non-existence of a peace to keep.

Canada provided 1,900 troops to Kabul in February 2003 (Pigott 2007, 92–93, 102). At the same time, the Department of Foreign Affairs and International Trade (DFAIT) sent a rebuilding team to Kabul. The Canadian International Development Agency (CIDA) arrived a month later, with the intention of implementing the Bonn Agreement (Windsor, Charters, and Wilson 2008, 11). By this time, Kabul constituted a deployment with limited danger, at least in comparison to the rest of Afghanistan. The Canadian mission to Kabul thus represented a pause in what had been a trend toward a greater combat role and also served Ottawa's intent to turn ISAF into a NATO operation.

NATO took over responsibility for the ISAF mission on 16 April 2003 (Stein and Lang 2007, 95). Germany's defence minister, Peter Struck, confirmed on 5 May 2003 that his country would secure Kabul airport (Stein and Lang 2007, 97). This announcement foreshadowed a series of mission-related restrictions by allies that would have the effect of making Canada more likely to assume a combat role as long as it stayed in Afghanistan. Ottawa, in contrast to Bonn and some other NATO capitals, had not put restrictions on deployment of the CF.[2] Thus it came as no surprise when Canada agreed to take overall command of ISAF, a role that became more significant as combat action intensified. Canada's allocation of 2,500 troops stood as the fourth largest at this time (Pigott 2007, 85).

While progress occurred in Kabul—the CF, for instance, built infrastructure—less secure locations presented a different story. Suicide attacks by insurgents increased in 2003. Some groups that had engaged in humanitarian assistance, such as the Red Cross, left Afghanistan as the violence increased during that year (Windsor, Charters, and Wilson 2008, 25, 26). These reactions—understandable given the circumstances—confirmed that the insurgency's best long-term strategy might be to undermine support for the coalition by preventing improvements in the Afghan way of life.

Canada, on 14 April 2004, extended its Afghan mission into the summer of 2005. Given limited casualties and public non-perception of a combat role for the CF, this action produced limited controversy at home. Partisanship contributed to the relatively low profile of the Afghan deployment because the centre-right Conservatives served as the Opposition at the time. The Tories, with a more positive disposition toward a traditional role for the military, had no inclination to criticize the Liberal government on at least this one issue.

Ongoing Canadian deployment in Kabul focused on getting ready for the Afghan national election in October 2004 (Granatstein and Oliver 2011, 5). Close to half of Afghan citizens voted in the September parliamentary elections. Moreover, the Afghan people voted in "massive numbers," in spite of Taliban threats and violence, and elected Hamid Karzai as president (Windsor, Charters, and Wilson 2008, 27). Karzai, with 55.4 percent of the vote, thereby became the first democratically selected head of state in Afghanistan's history. Even the negative side of the new voting process, which included accusations of fraud, had a positive element; on election day the UN set up a three-person panel as an immediate response to investigate the charges that had been made. The panel, on which a former Canadian diplomat served, had sufficient legitimacy to put an end to a boycott among some of the candidates who had been making the charges concerning electoral irregularities.

Concerns about the degree of integration and therefore the likely overall effectiveness of security and development efforts increased in spite of individual steps forward such as holding elections and build-ing infrastructure in Kabul. US leadership, in particular, had come to realize as 2004 progressed that "rising Taliban influence would not be defeated by military power alone but with the spread of aid, secur-ity, and good government. It was time to roll OEF and ISAF together, get the Taliban insurgency under control, and accelerate the pace of reconstruction" (Windsor, Charters, and Wilson 2008, 27). In a word, multilateral efforts to protect and build Afghanistan needed much more coordination.

Even on the purely military front, NATO exhibited ongoing problems with cooperation from its members regarding deployment. Toward the end of 2003, an incident occurred that would foreshadow more serious difficulties to come: NATO Secretary General George Robertson could not get a mere six helicopters for Afghanistan even after going public with his request (Stein and Lang 2007, 100). This problem went beyond resources and into cooperation at a more general level. General Hillier (2010, 289; see also Travers and Owen 2008, 694–700), for example, refers to an ongoing lack of team effort, with each NATO member building its own "fiefdom."[3] This tendency created a number of other problems, over and above the challenge it posed for implementing any overall strategy against the insurgency. For instance, governments taking on the burden of combat resented a lack of uniform rules of engage-ment. National caveats, as restrictions on deployment became known, caused escalating tensions within the coalition.[4] This problem paralleled the lack of integration regarding PRTs and reinforced the sense of an overall absence of coordination within ISAF.

Not by coincidence did General Hillier receive appointment as CDS on 4 February 2005 (Stein and Lang 2007, 150–52). Paul Martin, the new prime minister, wanted progress in Afghanistan and saw the general as a man of action. At the centre-right of the Liberal Party, Martin showed greater openness than his predecessor as prime minister, the centre-left Chrétien, to a shift in security policy. Martin had been waiting in the wings for over a decade, so it also is possible that he welcomed the opportunity to put some distance between himself and the policies of Chrétien, who many supporters of Martin had seen as overstaying his welcome.[5]

Developments came swiftly from Ottawa, most notably in increasing resources and qualitatively different military deployments. Defence Minister Bill Graham announced on 13 February 2005 that Canada would move from Kabul to Kandahar. Hillier's Defence Policy Statement (DPS) called for Three-Block War: a unified approach, with interoperability and more money (Stein and Lang 2007, 155). "The 3-D approach, or what I preferred to call a team Canada mission," as Hillier (2010, 389) described it, regarded failed or failing governments as "not a security, governance or economic problem; it was all three, and had to be approached with that in mind." Armed with the DPS and his "forceful, optimistic personality," Hillier stimulated "an important psychological shift both within the Canadian Forces and in the government's view of the military" (Stein and Lang 2007, 157). Something beyond the uncertain quasi-combat role of the CF as it had developed since 9/11 now became more likely if not certain.

While its key events took place behind closed doors in Ottawa rather than on a battlefield, 21 March 2005 turned out to be a fateful day for Canada's involvement in Afghanistan. Martin met with Hillier and other key advisors about a range of foreign policy issues. Afghanistan quickly came to the fore. Hillier made a case for a battle group, with at least a thousand soldiers, and convinced the prime minister to provide that and approve of a shift from Kabul to combat in the much more dangerous south (Schiller 2006). General Hillier "strongly favoured the redeployment in order to give the Canadian Armed Forces an opportunity to engage in combat and thus play a role similar to that of the US and British forces" (Holland 2009, 11). In addition, the DFAIT preferred Kandahar as well. Thus Martin's government shifted in 2005 to a "war fighting mission" (Granatstein and Oliver 2011, 77). The CF had a green light for combat action when the situation might arise—something guaranteed to happen with a redeployment to southern Afghanistan.

Canadian efforts toward nation building accelerated at the same time. While PRTs had existed as a concept from the Bonn Agreement onward, implementation beyond Kabul stalled because of political infighting among NATO members. Canadian leadership conceived of PRTs "as a way to integrate diplomats, development officials, military assets, and police officers to address the causes of instability, namely poor governance, weak institutions, insurgency, regional warlords, and poverty" (Horn 2010, 21; see also Holland 2010, 277; CSPC 2008, 22). Cabinet approved Kandahar as the Canadian PRT site in May 2005. The Kandahar City PRT started operations at Camp Nathan Smith in August of that year (Holland 2010, 280, 281; Horn 2010, 21). This PRT featured 220 soldiers, along with a very small number of personnel from CIDA, DFAIT, and the Royal Canadian Mounted Police (Day 2010, 135).

PRTs fought a different kind of battle than direct combat, but the line between civilian and military activity blurred as the war progressed. Activities for the Canadians in Kandahar soon went beyond physical construction and included "creating a new provincial government as well as local councils so that the voice of the people could be heard" (Windsor, Charters, and Wilson 2008, 43). CF met with Afghan civilians in local *shuras*, consistent with the Afghan custom of informal gatherings held while seated on mats, in an attempt to build trust through regular communication.[6] Providing local leaders with an opportunity to voice opinions represented a key element in the ongoing effort to counteract the Taliban's intimidation tactics.

Not surprisingly, Taliban commanders feared that enhanced communication, along with reconstruction, would erode support for their cause. They targeted PRTs from the outset, so protection of development and reconstruction activities became a priority for the CF.

PRT efforts faced a number of obstacles, however, over and beyond Taliban violence. Based on his experience, Captain Tony Petrilli, a CF reservist, cited "deep mistrust" of the corrupt Afghan government and "military realities" taking precedence over reconstruction efforts (quoted in Pigott 2007, 146, 148). This problem comes up many times in studies of the Afghan war: an unfortunate but necessary trade-off between deployment of finite resources to improving security on the one hand versus nation building on the other. While both activities are necessary, security necessarily precedes the possibility of reconstruction efforts. Yet an Afghan population living at the edge of subsistence, and with many bad experiences from prior foreign interventions, would be hard pressed to believe that somehow the coalition's activities boded well for them in the absence of more immediate and observable improvements.

This dynamic created pressure on the Canadian mission—a race against time to provide enough benefits from reconstruction to gain and build upon at least minimal trust. Even the ability to provide security itself depended at least in part on a more trusting relationship with the Afghan people. For example, rooting out the insurgency could proceed much more effectively with intelligence about the identities and locations of Taliban fighters and especially commanders. The ability of the Taliban to blend in so effectively with their surroundings put a premium on information at the village level.

Perhaps most frequently cited as a problem area by those with on-the-ground experience is the condition of the ANP. Among persistent difficulties noted are corruption; illiteracy; inferior training, equipment, and pay; questionable loyalty; sudden departures for Islamic religious reasons; and limited trust (Pigott 2007, 136, 176). PRTs concentrated their efforts toward bringing the police force up to speed, but could make only limited progress. Lack of professionalism on the part of the ANP created guilt by association—a reputational problem for the coalition and Afghan government.

The date 29 June 2005 marked CF deployment to Kandahar Airfield (Pigott 2007, 105). That month also brought a marked increase in suicide bombings (Stein and Lang 2007, 201). Suicide attacks focused on inflicting casualties reflected the insurgency's adaptability to the latest enemy. Through this tactic the Taliban's leadership hoped to reach its real target: Canadian voters. According to one observer, the Canadian media "is almost certainly the major conduit between the enemy and the Canadian public" (Day 2010, 178). The Taliban had been losing in conventional military engagements and thus opened up a different front in the ongoing effort to drive out its Canadian adversary.

Operation Athena had come to an effective end on 18 October 2005 when the CF withdrew from Kabul (Horn 2010, 21).[7] NATO foreign ministers met in Brussels on 8 December 2005 to assess needs in security and reconstruction. A plan to expand ISAF's activities in Afghanistan came out of this meeting. Notably, ISAF would deploy more in the hotly contested southern provinces, with Canada in a leading role.

Soon after the NATO conference, a more inclusive collection of governments met to assess priorities for development. This gathering might be viewed as a sequel to the meeting that produced the Bonn Agreement at the outset of the new Afghanistan's existence. From a meeting in London, between 31 January and 1 February 2006, came the Afghanistan Compact. Canada figured prominently among the list of 60 participating governments that agreed to coordinate rebuilding efforts through the Compact's Afghan National Development Strategy. The Compact specified priorities as well as values for the Afghan government; it announced that "eliminating the narcotics industry" would be a vital area of work and that "men and women have equal rights and responsibilities" (Afghanistan Compact 2006, 2). Security emerged as an encompassing concept: "It requires good governance, justice and the rule of law, reinforced by reconstruction and development" (Afghanistan Compact 2006, 3). An understanding of the synergy between security and development comes through quite clearly here.

Ambitious in terms of governance are the Compact's further priorities regarding provision of basic services throughout the country and a "zero-tolerance policy towards official corruption" (Afghanistan Compact 2006, 3, 4). The Compact also enumerated specific benchmarks for infrastructure and natural resources: roads, air transport, energy, mining and natural resources, water resource management, urban development, and the environment. The document listed similar goals for education, health, agriculture and rural development, social protection, economic governance, and private sector development (Afghanistan Compact 2006, 9–12). PRTs would carry out such activities in reconstruction as a complement to military efforts toward greater security.

While full of good intentions, the Compact revealed some problems regarding the mindset among participants. The contents of the document show little understanding of how long-established values in Afghanistan might conflict with near-sacred principles in advanced countries ranging from gender equality to freedom from corruption. This Compact, moreover, also shows only a minimal grasp of just how much time and money would be involved in any effort to turn Afghanistan from chaos into a functional country.

Intense military engagements in 2006, with Canada in a major role, represented a reality that looked very different from the one envisioned by the Afghanistan Compact at the outset of that year. Operation Archer, the sequel to Athena, got underway in February 2006 (Horn 2010, 22). The new operation would seek enclaves of Taliban fighters and clear them out at a village level. CF units transferred from ISAF to a coordinated effort with US troops in Kandahar under the auspices of OEF. This promised to increase, in at least an incremental way, the CF's role in the fighting. After a shift in government during the Canadian election at the outset of 2006, political developments proved crucial in ensuring that the CF's movement toward full-fledged combat would find backing from Ottawa.

Stephen Harper became Canada's twenty-second prime minister on 6 February 2006. His rise to power represented a major change in Canadian politics, even with just a minority government at the outset. A Conservative, Harper came from Alberta and had a Western power base. He emerged from a more programmatically conservative ideological foundation than previous Tory prime ministers.[8] This included openness to a more traditional role for the CF as opposed to the peace-making entity that had become established under a series of preceding governments from both parties.

Consider the mindset that greeted Harper as he took office. By March 2006, only 27.7 percent of Canadians understood Afghanistan to be a combat mission (Fletcher, Bastedo, and Hove 2009, 920). This number is interesting to ponder, especially in light of events on 15 January 2006. On that date a suicide bombing attack killed a Canadian diplomat, Glyn Berry (head of the PRT's foreign affairs section), and injured three soldiers (Sjolander 2009, 87; Windsor, Charters, and Wilson 2008, 44). An ingrained sense of peacekeeping almost certainly biased the Canadian public against a realization that Afghanistan represented something fundamentally different for the CF.

With time, however, greater public consciousness of the implications from casualties took hold. By the spring of 2006, "the growing Canadian casualty count, and the media coverage surrounding each death, created a public environment in which meaningful debate over Afghanistan seemed impossible to avoid—despite the prime minister's best efforts" (Sjolander 2009, 87; see also Windsor, Charters, and Wilson 2008, xviii).[9] These reactions show the power of the psychological environment in place as the reality of Canadian involvement in war mounted. Even very limited casualties created the perception of major losses—greatly reduced from the capacity to absorb damage exhibited by the Canadian public in previous wartime experiences. Canadians had become used to rare and even then usually accidental loss of life from peacekeeping. They reacted with shock to single-digit casualty reports because of the qualitative change inherent in such news. Combat losses signalled activity that many had assumed to be a thing of the past.

Harper soon introduced a political debate, which initially came as a great surprise, on Afghanistan. While on the surface the war seemed like a point of vulnerability for the minority government, at a deeper level things worked differently. Harper knew that, while his own party stood united in favour of continuing, the Liberal Party, his principal adversary for control of government, had significant divisions over the deployment in Afghanistan (Sjolander 2009, 88). The internal conflict among Grits would be certain to come out in a public debate and therefore, if handled in the right way, could work in his favour. Thus a government motion in Parliament, on 15 May 2006, proposed to extend the Afghanistan mission to 2009. The Tory government permitted just two days of debate, with the vote to be held on 17 May 2006. The motion passed 149 to 145, a result that reflected mixed public views on the subject. Support for the Afghan war hovered at around 50 percent during the year (Kirton and

Guebert 2007, 16; see also Stein and Lang 2007, 239–41). As Harper had expected, the Liberals in Parliament had a very difficult time managing the issue, with some supporting the motion and others not. The prime minister effectively managed to have his cake and eat it, too: keeping the war effort underway while weakening the Opposition.

Canadian engagements in Afghanistan, which certainly met the description of a war, began to have ripple effects. Canada, for instance, announced on 28 June 2006 the purchase of Chinook helicopters. This would make the CF less dependent on allies for troop movements and showed a serious intention to improve the situation on the ground in Afghanistan. The acquisition also reflected the momentum of Canadian commitment to the war after years of involvement.

Battles conducted under the auspices of Operation Archer took on a greater scale than before.[10] Major engagements took place in the Panjwayi region during the summer of 2006. Panjwayi is located in the Kandahar Province and figured prominently into the strategy of the Taliban leader Mullah Dadullah Akhund to win a symbolic victory. Intelligence reports indicated that he hoped to surround Kandahar City and would intensify actions leading up to August 19, Afghanistan's national Independence Day. The Taliban knew their fighters ultimately would be driven out of Kandahar; they just wanted "international television cameras to be there" (Wattie 2008, 42–43). It would be a major victory for the Taliban to conduct visible operations in the vicinity of Kandahar, regardless of the specific tactical outcomes that resulted from battles fought against coalition forces.

Canada responded proactively to intelligence reports about the forthcoming Taliban offensive. Canadian Lieutenant Colonel Ian Hope assembled what became known as Task Force (TF) Orion (i.e., for the constellation named after a hunter). The name is revealing because it symbolizes how CF deployment had evolved from a defensive posture to a more active sense of protection for development efforts—seeking out and fighting the Taliban who put PRTs and Afghan civilians at risk. The TF relied on light armoured vehicles—"eight-wheeled, lightly armoured infantry vehicles" with a "small auto-cannon and a machine gun that delivered accurate fire from under armour protection"—to keep the roads open (Windsor, Charters, and Wilson 2008, 47). Orion also had the 11 Field Engineer Squadron for dealing with IEDs, building fortifications, and repairing roads.[11] Together, the light armoured vehicle–based units and engineers played a key role in making it possible for PRTs to operate in the dangerous Kandahar region. By the time of its deployment, according to an embedded journalist, TF Orion had become a "killing machine" (Blatchford 2008, 2).

TF Orion had a challenging assignment for the summer fighting season of 2006: "move into Pashmul, the western edge of the notoriously sketchy Panjwaii [Panjwayi] area just thirty kilometres west of Kandahar, and clear out the Taliban" (Blatchford 2008, 70). Hope's TF fought a number of engagements against the Taliban, within which the CF acquitted itself quite well. Of special note are the adverse conditions under which these and most other battles with insurgents took place: fighting resumed in the spring after a winter hiatus and generally included extremely hot weather conditions. Soldiers fought the risk of dehydration and exhaustion every bit as much as the Taliban. The setting also included many natural hiding places for Taliban fighters, most notably huge thick-walled buildings intended for the drying of grapes into raisins. These structures served as very effective places from which to launch attacks; even the use of artillery often failed to penetrate the massive walls of dried mud.

Battles at Bayanji on May 16 and 17 and Seyyedin on June 12 entailed fierce fighting. During one engagement a suicide bomber had been taken out before being able to kill any Canadian soldiers—a major accomplishment that received no media coverage (Blatchford 2008, 32). In addition, a brigade attack at one point marked the first time in memory that US infantry had been under the operational control of a Canadian military officer (Blatchford 2008, 214). Developments such as these reveal the major changes being experienced by the CF both in activity and reputation. It would have been unthinkable, for instance, for US forces to serve in battle under Canadian command before the mettle of the CF had been tested so thoroughly.

CF's Charlie Company, which came to be nicknamed Contact Charlie because of its battle experience, saw considerable action. Perhaps most memorable among the military engagements for Contact Charlie, the battle at the White Schoolhouse on August 3 took place in gruelling conditions. By 10:30 a.m. the temperature already had reached nearly 50 degrees Celsius. Around 11:30 a.m., hundreds of Taliban fighters attacked eight Canadian infantrymen. The ensuing three-hour battle resulted in four Canadians killed and much greater losses for the Taliban. TF Orion's assaults on the White and Yellow Schoolhouses resulted in three Taliban commanders killed and others wounded, along with dozens of fighters wounded or captured. In sum, the battle ended in a victory for the CF.

While successful in an immediate sense, these battles established that more Taliban had moved into Panjwayi than any intelligence reports had indicated. This constituted a direct challenge to ISAF. As described by Colonel Bernd Horn (2010, 31), ISAF had been following an "ink spot method" in fighting the Taliban. Creating secure areas and then expanding and connecting them represented the underlying goal of military engagements; this drew on "the method of state-building and counter-insurgency employed successfully by the British in Malaya in the 1950s" (Windsor, Charters, and Wilson 2008, 90). The Taliban understood this strategy and tried at all costs to prevent any given area from staying safe for long enough to give it a sense of permanence.

TF Orion completed its mission in August 2006. Its final month of activity, interestingly enough, took place after a transfer of command from Operation Archer back to Operation Athena. Thus at least some of the heavy fighting took place under the auspices of ISAF and NATO as opposed to Canadian cooperation with the US alone.

Escalating military engagements revealed an additional complication that followed from the CF's prior existence as a non-fighting entity. Military bureaucrats, considerably removed from the location of fighting, in some instances intervened directly regarding missions and tactics (Blatchford 2008, 4).[12]

Operation Medusa began for the CF on 2 September 2006. A major ISAF offensive, assisted by the ANA, Operation Medusa spanned 1 September to 17 September 2006. It focused on Panjwayi, an enemy stronghold, 30 kilometres from Kandahar City (Horn 2010, 11, 12). A major battle occurred at the White Schoolhouse Complex on September 3 and bombardment of the Taliban took its toll from September 6 to September 10 (Horn 2010, 66–67, 104). This assault on the Taliban stronghold in Pashmul ultimately succeeded through firepower and persistence. The venture entailed heavy casualties for Charlie Company in particular. Objective Rugby, in the Panjwayi district of Kandahar Province, constituted the largest Canadian-led battle in more than half a century (Day 2010, 74).

All things considered, Operation Medusa represented a "major tactical defeat" for the Taliban (Stein and Lang 2007, 220; CSPC 2008, 19). Yet key concerns arose in the aftermath. For one, quite a few Taliban escaped and thus could and did return to attack Kandahar at other points (Horn 2010, 117; Wattie 2008, 218–32). For another, Taliban came back to the same ground later because the coalition lacked the forces to hold it (CSPC 2008, 23). Members of TF Orion expressed frustration at the need to keep taking the same ground in the Panjwayi–Pashmul area (Blatchford 2008, 338).

While the ANA participated, the CF took on most of the fighting in this offensive (Horn 2010, 12). On the one hand, the action revealed a reinvigoration of the Canadian military. From the standpoint of a participant, Operation Medusa represented "an epic combat engagement" and "a significant Canadian benchmark. It signaled to Canadians and allies that Canada was once again ready to engage its personnel in combat operations" (Horn 2010, 13). On the other hand, combat triggered underlying resistance among Canadians at home. Casualties from Operation Medusa stimulated "public emotionalism" (Granatstein and Oliver 2011, 6; see also Windsor, Charters, and Wilson 2008, 55). Harper knew that war fighting in principle and Afghanistan in practice faced significant opposition, which included marginal voters who would be crucial in any future election. The prime minister thus had to acknowledge publicly for the first time, in September 2006, that Canada was fighting a war in Afghanistan.

Harper understood that his minority government could fall if adversaries in Parliament saw an opportunity to mobilize and win on the basis of skepticism about Canadians in combat. When the New Democratic Party (NDP) called for a quick withdrawal and the polls showed that support for the war had declined, the prime minister revealed anything but a tin ear. Harper responded with a state visit intended to show Afghanistan in its best light. President Karzai visited Ottawa and Montreal from 21 September to 23 September 2006. As the prime minister would have hoped, a poll right after the visit showed 57 percent support for the war among Canadians (Pigott 2007, 127). The Karzai visit, in spite of its possible short-term impact on opinion, also pointed toward an ongoing need to justify Canada's involvement in a war that already had been underway for what seemed to the public like a very long time.

Military engagements occurred at a reduced level during the fall and winter months of 2006–7. Canada brought in Leopard tanks toward the end of 2006 to protect PRT convoys (Pigott 2007, 189). On the one hand, this represented a positive development in terms of improved safety for CF personnel. On the other hand, it pointed to the intensifying attacks that created the need for more heavily armoured vehicles to protect PRT activities. The insurgents, as noted earlier, increasingly focused their efforts on inflicting casualties and disrupting reconstruction (Horn 2010, 122). A shift to the use of IEDs in particular reflected the continuing success of the CF and its allies in military operations against Taliban strongholds. In December 2006, for example, Operation Falcon Summit, north of Panjwayi, chased out insurgents and enabled the building of a new road that would facilitate PRT efforts.

TF-107 deployed to Afghanistan from February through August 2007. On the development front, Canadian efforts to rebuild Kandahar had gained momentum by the spring of 2007. CIDA "worked to establish municipal councils and manage the first public works projects that rural Kandaharis had seen in decades, if ever" (Windsor, Charters, and

Wilson 2008, xix, xx). Emphasis had been placed on Kandahar City in particular: "the PRT devoted a lot of attention to restoring basic city services, training municipal government, getting young people into schools, and paving the way for businesses to get back on their feet" (Windsor, Charters, and Wilson 2010, 100). Progress in this instance reveals how security and reconstruction are so closely intertwined. First, military operations taking place in the Helmand Valley, in particular, drew fire away from rebuilding efforts in Kandahar. Second, at a community level, significant numbers of young men hired to work had been Tier 2 Taliban fighters (Windsor, Charters, and Wilson 2008, 104, 123).

May 2007 showed a substantial presence for ISAF and the ANA in the "most populous and strategically important" part of Kandahar (Windsor, Charters, and Wilson 2008, 177).[13] The insurgency, which continued to be seasonal, had not picked up until late spring. Its ability to resume fighting in a full-fledged way revealed the firm foundation of the Taliban in Kandahar (Windsor, Charters, and Wilson 2008, 87, 88). By June, however, the "mood in Panjwayi changed" and the Taliban moved elsewhere; previously dangerous areas even enjoyed relative safety during the night (Windsor, Charters, and Wilson 2008, 190, 205).

TF-107, en route from Route Summit to western Zharey district and beyond, had a key purpose: "to dominate that vital oasis and create a security zone around the most populous areas where the Provincial Reconstruction Team, the Afghan government, and aid agencies needed to work" (Windsor, Charters, and Wilson 2008, 89). If this difficult challenge could be met, PRTs could continue their efforts in the Afghan Development Zone. Progress there, in turn, would give Afghan citizens a more attractive option than joining or supporting the insurgency in other ways. Thus, once again, security and reconstruction are seen to depend on each other.

Military action against the Taliban to support the PRT effort, but without collateral damage, stood as the basic purpose of TF-107. The TF succeeded. The fight in Siah Choy, like others, did not harm civilians. A battle on June 20 at Howz-e-Madad, on the northern side of the Arghandab River, produced no Afghan casualties. Fighting continued in July and once again did not harm civilians during the process of clearing out insurgents and facilitating reconstruction (Windsor, Charters, and Wilson 2008, 185, 187).

Something should be said here about the reasons behind the extraordinary success of the CF in averting loss of civilian life in particular and collateral damage in general as the war progressed. In a situation in which it could prove so difficult to distinguish combatants from others, this stands as a great accomplishment (Horn 2010, 124, 131).

An ability to prevent civilian casualties while maintaining combat effect-iveness became built into CF training: "the process of readying TF-107 took more time than the actual mission itself" (Windsor, Charters, and Wilson 2008, 59). Before TF-107 deployed, for instance, Afghan-Canadians helped its members to prepare for action on the ground. This training proved invaluable "for troops headed into an isolated Islamic society that viewed all foreigners with suspicion and where leading by example of good behaviour was critical to winning the respect and faith of Afghans" (Windsor, Charters, and Wilson 2008, 76, 77, 79, 163).

All parties to the conflict understood collateral damage to be the source of anger that would produce new insurgents. Thus the CF's sustained ability to hunt down the Taliban and fight battles against them without civilian casualties had both offensive and defensive value. IED attacks, such as the fatal one on July 4, became the insurgency's preferred method of fighting out of necessity. The Taliban launched more than 140 suicide bombings in 2007 (CSPC 2008, 17). This made sense in light of the CF's performance in more conventional battles. Even the best Taliban fighters could not match the tactics and firepower of the Canadian units. Instead, the insurgents harassed reconstruction efforts; their leaders hoped that CF casualties would erode support in Canada for the war effort.

Public opposition to the war continued to grow (CSPC 2008, 17). In January 2008, the report from the Independent Panel on Canada's Future Role in Afghanistan, headed by John Manley, the highly experienced former cabinet minister and deputy prime minister within the Chrétien government, became available. This non-partisan document contains a vast amount of information and opinion; it stands as undoubtedly the most comprehensive and influential report during the war. While not without positive observations regarding the war, the Independent Panel (2008, 13) identified a range of ongoing and serious challenges:

> The most damaging shortfalls include an insufficiency of forces in the field, especially in high-risk zones in the South; a top-heavy command structure at ISAF headquarters in Kabul, an absence of a comprehensive strategy directing all ISAF forces in collaboration with the Afghan government; limitations placed by some NATO governments on the operations of their units, which effectively keep those forces out of the conflict; and inadequate coordination between military and civilian programs for security, stabilization, reconstruction and development.

The Independent Panel (2008, 15, 13, 20) also expressed concerns about civilian casualties and the potential ability of the insurgency to win by simply outlasting its adversaries, along with an "information deficit" as a result of inadequate communication to Canadians from their government about the war's purpose.

These points, among others, are revisited in the assessment in Chapter 4 of the contemporary situation facing Canada in Afghanistan. The key operational point when the Independent Panel's report was released concerned its rejection of the existing end date for the Canadian military mission in Kandahar: "the Panel could find no operational logic for choosing February 2009" (Independent Panel 2008, 30). The Independent Panel also specified a series of options for government policy and found all of them wanting to some degree.

Observers have summed up the report from the Independent Panel, in light of how Harper acted on it, as "helpfully ambiguous" (Granatstein and Oliver 2011, 7). Sjolander (2009, 91) offers the following assessment:

> Canada's . . . continued presence should be increasingly focused on training the Afghan National Security Forces to take on a greater share of the security burden—with a concomitant diminution in Canada's combat role as the Afghan forces gained skills and experience.

The Independent Panel could see what had become more obvious with time: the views of Canadians and Afghans for the mission had converged, albeit with a limited shelf life. Canadian criticism occurred publicly through opposition parties and the media. Afghan opinion could be picked up in more subtle ways. For example, the insurgents' ability to implement IEDs so effectively established that at least some significant support existed for their efforts among the Afghan population (Day 2010, 190).

Soon after accepting the Independent Panel's report, Harper recommended extending Canada's role in Afghanistan to 2011. (In all likelihood he formed the Panel to obtain the extension.) This time around he did not face the same level of opposition; the House of Commons voted 191 to 77 on 13 March 2008 in favour of extending the mission. The confidence motion included an emphasis on training Afghan troops, along with reconstruction, and thus implicitly recognized the degree of mission fatigue that existed among the public. The motion also included a firm date for the CF to leave Kandahar: July 2011.

US infantry battalions began to arrive in August 2008 in support of the Canadians. While positive in one sense, this deployment also reflected, at least in part, continuing concerns about the ANA. In 2008, NATO assessed 62 percent of ANA units to be incapable of conducting "battalion-level operations with some ISAF support" (Chaudhuri and Farrell 2011, 274). CF members alone could not compensate for this lack of Afghan ability to take on military action independently. More troops would be needed and the US redeployed units from an improving Iraq to help with the struggle for southern Afghanistan.

Fighting throughout 2008–9 followed the pattern established over the previous few years. Coalition forces would clear areas of the Taliban and try to hold on so reconstruction could move ahead. Examples of operations from that period will be sufficient to make the point about continuity. August 2008 featured Operation Eagle Summit, a major coalition offensive in Helmand Province. CF joined in with troops from other NATO governments in battles that, once again, produced tactical success. The reconstruction-related goal of providing Helmand with electric power then moved ahead. In January 2009, Operation Shahi Tandar went forward in the Helmand and Kandahar Provinces. This off-season offensive destroyed a Taliban factory in the Kandahar Province that had been used to create IEDs. In a separate battle, CF in combination with other NATO troops cleared out the Taliban from what had been a stronghold in the vicinity of Spin Masjid. These actions proved typical over the course of a two-year period that might now be regarded as one of waiting. The coalition would require enhanced resources to facilitate action at a more strategic level against the insurgency.

Two points on the public relations front combined to reveal the ongoing challenge to Harper in selling the war to Canadians. First, the presidential elections of 2009 had been plagued by substantial fraud and this fed into existing suspicions about incurable corruption. Karzai's significant support told only part of the story: "the high approval rating for the President may reflect an inclination to support political authority and thus not provide an accurate picture of Karzai's personal popularity" (Chaudhuri and Farrell 2011, 286–87). The second issue concerned human rights and the conduct of the CF. Rumours regarding mistreatment of Afghan detainees spread, with Parliament hearing testimony in November 2009. Defence Minister Peter MacKay continued to voice the government's denial of the allegations, but the issue crept into public consciousness in spite of a lack of hard evidence. MacKay, in fact, replaced Defence Minister Gordon O'Connor, who ended up being demoted as the political scandal gained traction in the Canadian media.

Harper continued to support the war effort in spite of such challenges. Given the difficulties noted, rather than selling the war, the prime minister seemed to be trying to keep it off the public agenda to the greatest extent possible. Harper increased the military budget (Granatstein and Oliver 2011, 190). While various critics had called for an even greater infusion of resources, the $20 billion increase represented a considerable amount of money under existing political conditions. Consider the scope of the Canadian role in Afghanistan by early 2010 (Granatstein and Oliver 2011, 6):

> the size and complexity of the Kandahar mission was indicated by its organizational structure, which included command and headquarters staff, an air force contingent, helicopters and unmanned aerial vehicles (drones), intelligence and communications troops, special forces, mentor and liaison teams working with Afghan military and paramilitary units, an infantry battalion, a tank squad, armoured reconnaissance troops, military police, an artillery battery, an engineer squadron, medical personnel, and substantial numbers of American infantry.

This role—almost beyond belief for the Canada of just a few short years ago—included operational military and reconstruction components. These activities had become symbiotic as the war progressed.

December 2009 brought the announcement by President Barack Obama of a major surge: 30,000 additional troops would deploy to Afghanistan. This would have significant implications for the CF as it waited for the next summer fighting season. Operation Moshtarak (the Dari word for "together"), the largest offensive of the war, would get underway soon after US reinforcements arrived. It involved approximately 15,000 military personnel from the coalition and ANA. Operation Moshtarak focused on Helmand Province, adjacent to Kandahar. The operation intended to disrupt the activities of drug traffickers and the Taliban, which still operated with impunity in some locations, most notably Marja. Weakening the opium trade would strike directly at insurgent financing and thus the subsequent ability to attack. Crucial to success for Operation Moshtarak would be the performance of the ANA. Afghan forces would play a central role that might be viewed as a dress rehearsal for later, more independent combat action. Canadian units and others from the coalition had invested significant time in training, so this would be a major test of ANA readiness.

Operation Moshtarak got underway on 13 February 2010 (Holland and Kirkey 2010, 67). Helicopters deployed coalition forces before dawn that day. While US and ANA forces entered Marja, CF and other coalition members attacked in the Nad Ali district. As with other military operations, the coalition succeeded in a tactical sense. Deployments met all objectives either on the day of the attacks or soon after.

However, by the summer of 2010, the Taliban revealed a significant residual presence in the areas it ceded to the coalition in battle. Sporadic violence continued and insurgents intimidated local residents who cooperated with the coalition. Once again, while unsuccessful in battle, the Taliban capably resisted efforts at reconstruction. This also successfully removed the feasibility of destroying the poppy fields that produced income for the insurgency. Without safe and reliable alternatives for income, farmers simply would be enraged by poppy eradication and become likely recruits for the insurgency. Taken together, Operation Moshtarak, like other operations before it, can be viewed as a success but only at a tactical level.

Chapter 4

A New Postwar Canadian Identity

How and Why?

After years of fighting, how did Afghans view the war? Survey data from the International Council on Security and Development (2011) proves quite revealing about public opinion in Afghanistan. While allowing for the challenges of carrying out survey research during wartime conditions, the results in Table 4-1 have an authentic ring to them. The numbers conveyed by the table are based on responses from 125 male students at Kabul University in 2010.

Note that only a few questions produced one-sided percentages and all but two feature "No Answer/Don't Know" with percentages in double-figures. These properties reveal the controversy and uncertainty regarding any important question about Afghanistan, even in its most stable location and among relatively safe and educated people. The three questions about Osama bin Laden produce generally favourable results from a Canadian point of view: his passing is seen as a positive thing, with negative implications for the Taliban in Afghanistan. A slim margin, however, is in favour of seeing al Qaeda survive beyond its leader's death. Also positive are solid differences that appear in favour of military operations against the Taliban and a perception that foreign forces and the Afghan government are winning the war. However, note the margin in favour of a transition of foreign forces out of Afghanistan. This occurs even with overwhelming percentages of respondents saying that the Taliban is not respected in their community, that they would prefer to see it gone, and that working with the Taliban is wrong. Overall, the survey data seems to be saying that Afghans think the time for their own forces to take over from the coalition is at hand or even overdue.

Table 4-1   Public Opinion Data from Kabul

Question	Yes (%)	No (%)	No Answer/ Don't Know (%)
Is Osama bin Laden's death good news [i.e., "yes" answer] or bad news [i.e., "no" answer]?	58	36	6
Is al Qaeda finished now that Osama bin Laden is dead?	39	42	19
Does Osama bin Laden's death affect the Taliban and their fight in Afghanistan?	51	28	17 (additional 4% say it will help)
Do you support military operations against the Taliban in your area?	61	30	9
Who is winning the war? Foreign forces and the Afghan government ["yes" answer] or the Taliban ["no" answer]?	57	34	10[a]
Is it good ["yes" answer] or bad ["no" answer] that the foreign forces are starting this transition?	68	20	12
What is the status of the Taliban in your community? ["yes" answer means they are respected; "no" answer means they are disrespected]	10	72	18
Do you want the Taliban to go ["yes" answer] or stay ["no" answer]?	66	5	29
Do you think that working with the Taliban is right ["yes" answer] or wrong ["no" answer]?	6	74	20

Source: Adapted from International Council on Security and Development 2011
[a]Numbers exceed 100 percent due to rounding.

Canadian actions at the time of writing are in tune with likely Afghan sentiments regarding the intervention. Combat troops departed in the summer of 2011 and withdrawal of CF assets from Kandahar Province was completed by the end of that year (Sachs 2011; DFAIT 2011g). Afghan soldiers and police mentored by the CF are working closely with US troops in new military operations scheduled for Kandahar (DFAIT 2011g). For example, an offensive over two weeks in June, south of the Arghandab River, had 50 percent Afghans among 3,000 personnel. Planned and executed by CF-trained Afghan troops, the operation represented "a point of pride for officers of the Canadian task force in Kandahar" (Sachs 2011). Signs of transition to the ANA are clear; for example, CF in Kabul have started to participate in the NATO-based training mission, scheduled to last until March 2014 (DFAIT 2011g).

Characteristics of Canadian involvement in Afghanistan may be summed up via the heading of a section from the preceding chapter: in, out, and back in again. Canada joined in, to the extent its limited military capabilities permitted, with the initial US invasion of Afghanistan. Canada then backed off, as would be expected from its background, which was conveyed in Chapter 2. Canadians, however, came back into Afghanistan and played a major role in both fighting and reconstruction until 2011. Why did this pattern occur? Perspectives based on the government and domestic politics, realism, liberalism, and the world of ideas all have something to contribute here.

Incrementalism, derived from an outlook based on the government and domestic politics, is the conventional account (Stein and Lang 2007). Canadian leaders are regarded as entering into major combat action one decision at a time, with the net result looking quite different than what anyone would have intended at the outset. "The decision to have the Canadian Forces fight for the United States in this dangerous counter-insurgency role," as described by Lennox (2009, 96), "was not made in a linear, rational manner." To begin, consider the reinvigorated role in Afghanistan as a safeguard against going into Iraq (Sjolander 2009, 85; Dyment 2010, 42; Hillier 2010, 262). To go back into Afghanistan under the auspices of NATO in ISAF seemed like the best way to "ensure an exit strategy for the CF" (Stein and Lang 2007, 66). However, this decision also created momentum. It functioned, in effect, as "the first step down a long road" (Stein and Lang 2007, 72).

PRTs can be seen in the same light. In theory, they were a way of limiting commitment, but in practice, they were anything but part of an exit strategy (Stein and Lang 2007, 108). On the surface, these operations would seem innocuous vis-à-vis any challenge to Canada's self-image as a peacekeeper. However, with whatever words might be preferred—perhaps *mission creep* might be suitable here—PRT activity soon transcended what Canadians had understood as traditional peacekeeping and nation building. Reconstruction in an active war zone would require military security and entail combat operations. Thus the decision to become involved in PRTs represented another step down the road toward fighting a war.

Once involved with PRTs, Canada's participation in US-led missions to seek out and fight the Taliban directly would not be far off. The highly interdependent nature of security and development in both theoretical and operational terms produced that result. Active defence of reconstruction teams would point toward proactive measures to eliminate the insurgent threat before it could harm PRTs and Afghan civilians. As summed up by Stein and Lang (2007, 244), it is "almost always far easier to get in than it is to get out." Bureaucratic inertia, from this point of view, explains how the process unfolded: "Canada slipped into war in Afghanistan, step by step, incrementally, without fully understanding that it was going to war, until it woke up to mounting casualties and grim battles" (Stein and Lang 2007, 244). Along those lines, consider the words of former DFAIT minister Lloyd Axworthy: "War has its own momentum. The deeper you get into it, the more you tend to lose sight of your objectives" (quoted in Schiller 2006).

This inertial model of Canada in Afghanistan, derived from an outlook based on the government and domestic politics, finds support in the specific context of the Canadian decision to stay out of Iraq. Reconstruction of US and Canadian decision making establishes that Washington had not been pressuring Ottawa into a military role in the Iraq War. At least in publicly available accounts, evidence suggests the opposite. It appears that the US hoped for political, rather than military, support from Canada for the Iraq War (Stein and Lang 2007, 46–51). With the likelihood that the US knew about limited Canadian military capabilities, this preference borders on certainty. The US had a public relations issue with its imminent invasion of Iraq, for which neither NATO nor UN endorsement had been forthcoming. Given Canada's steadfast support for multilateralism and generally positive reputation in the world, it makes all the more sense that Washington would have been looking for Ottawa's blessing more than anything else. The misperception of pressure from Washington supports the momentum thesis in at least an indirect way; Canadian leaders seemed disposed toward greater commitment and therefore tended to read the tea leaves on that basis.

Dey (2011, 2–3) offers a pointed critique of the inertial or momentum-based argument. She challenges the standard account, derived from the perspective of the government and domestic politics and conveyed by Stein and Lang (2007), about the evolving Canadian role in Afghanistan: "Positioning Rick Hillier as protagonist, they argue that the military, a group that believed that Canada needed to pledge support to the Americans, came to dominate Canada's foreign policy agenda and, as a result, Canada ended up deeper in Afghanistan than it originally had intended."[1] Other scholars also point to a possibly exaggerated role for Hillier at the centre of a largely bureaucratic story about military deployment. "Richard Arbeiter, Deputy Director of Policy on the Afghanistan Task Force at the Department of Foreign Affairs," according to Windsor, Charters, and Wilson (2008, 35), "balks at the idea that Gen. Hillier drove the Kandahar commitment." Arbeiter instead emphasized a gradual process of approval of Cabinet recommendations on implementing PRTs and adding combat forces. Moreover, other officials dispute that Hillier wanted to go into a dangerous area such as Kandahar to impress the US (Windsor, Charters, and Wilson 2008, 35).

Part of the momentum-based story, of course, remains intact even in this critique; notice that the words *gradual process* figure prominently here. The unflattering and even reckless role attributed to General Hillier, however, is disputed directly. Instead, the alternative view offered by Windsor, Charters, and Wilson (2008, 37) emphasizes "well-intentioned" decision making in Ottawa with follow-up in terms of money and personnel toward implementation.

Dey (2011, 3) argues that neither incrementalism, which pushes the role of bureaucracy, nor realism, which emphasizes material interests, can provide a convincing explanation for how Canada's role in Afghanistan changed in specific ways. She calls instead for an account based on the world of ideas. The key gap in understanding the characteristics of Canadian involvement is this one: "no analysis has grappled with how material facts acquired meaning in Canada's decisions regarding Afghanistan" and thus a new focus is needed to identify the "mechanism through which Canada conceived of threat" (Dey 2011, 3, 4). An emphasis on incrementalism and bureaucratically induced momentum misses the underlying causes. As with the initial decision to take on a military role in late 2001, the Canadian choice to expand its role significantly in 2005 created a dynamic that could not easily be reversed. The policy change in favour of a war-fighting stance altered even further the mindset that had existed in both Canadian government and society about their role in the world. Thus momentum existed, and might even be traced through bureaucratic decision making, but new *ideas* constituted the engine that moved things in a different direction. Human security steadily lost ground to national security both in policy and the public mind.

Policy documents, such as the Defence Policy Statement (DPS) from 2005, conveyed government positions at variance from previous ones that focused on human security: "Gone were references to the CF's role in traditional peacekeeping missions; instead, the *DPS* suggested that the CF's future would be 'far more complex and dangerous,' and focused on failed and failing countries where 'there is little if any peace to keep'" (Dey 2011, 31). Herein lies the key difference from the account offered by Stein and Lang (2007), which had emphasized the leadership of Hillier in a world of incrementalism and bureaucratic drift. Hillier, instead, articulated ideas that struck a chord with Prime Minister Martin's vision for Canada's role in the world (Dey 2011, 30).

Canada, according to an account based on ideas, had started to process material data differently under the leadership of the new prime minister. By 2005, it had moved away from a focus on the security of individuals. Instead, the Canadian government turned to a perception of failing and failed states as a threat to national or state-level security (Dey 2011, 43). The election of Harper, with an ideologically conservative position, opened the door to an even more realist-oriented foreign policy.

Take, for instance, the position put forward in *Managing Turmoil*, a Senate Committee report from 2006. Written as Canadian wartime commitments neared their peak (ultimately up to 3,000 troops in 2010–11), the report urges the government to make a commitment to national defence over and above whatever is politically expedient (Canada 2006b, 11). The Senate Committee calls for a doubling of the Department of National Defence (DND) budget, from 1 to 2 percent, because instability around the world soon will turn the current Canadian sense of security into nothing more than an illusion (Canada 2006b, 16, 23). These elements of the report clearly follow from realist thinking; if you want peace, prepare for war.

Previously established norms regarding human security, however, are not absent from this report. The Senate Committee also calls for a doubling of the foreign aid budget of $2.7 billion from 0.36 to 0.7 percent of GDP; the latter figure would be in line with what the World Bank's Pearson Commission had recommended in September 1969 (Canada 2006b, 24, 25). This type of spending is clearly more in line with a vision of responsibility toward those around the world in vulnerable positions. It might be fair to say that the middle of the decade featured a blending of established and new ideas in the Canadian mindset. A resurgent realism, with an emphasis on national security and pursuit of national interest understood in a more traditional way, challenged the hegemony of liberalism as theory and human security as practice in foreign policy.

Why did this change come about? As with entry into the war as described in Chapter 2, the idea-based perspective emphasizes the discourse among Canada's allies. Policy responses, in turn, shifted the identity underlying Canadian perception of national interests (Dey 2011, 9). At least from the perspective of those involved with Canadian decision making, the views of allies about Canadian commitment to defence, most notably in terms of military deployment, had come to matter a great deal. Consider the words of Scott Reid, former communications director for Prime Minister Paul Martin, in recalling how those involved in the shift to Kandahar and a war-fighting deployment felt in 2005: "There was a feeling that this was the price of being a G-8 country. . . . It was a question of, you know, having shown up all these years with a six-pack, whether we were finally going to tend bar" (Schiller 2006). Canada would need to embrace a foreign policy based on realist principles, under these circumstances, or run the risk of marginalization within the Western elite.

While the momentum-based interpretation of Canadian characteristics now seems limited, with elements of additional perspectives essential to explaining how events progressed, other aspects of government and domestic politics can help to achieve a more comprehensive account. The specific component introduced here is the media—perhaps the most important bridge between government and society. The media is criticized, from various quarters, as effectively supporting a liberal versus realist view on the war: "And while the media focused on more Canadian deaths in Afghanistan," observed Windsor, Charters, and Wilson (2008, 127–28), "no one covered the first ever Kandahar half-marathon that ran that very day; no stories were filed on the irrigation system restoration, or the road and culvert repairs that propelled the largest agricultural growth in southern Afghanistan in a decade. Nothing that gave meaning to those deaths made the headlines in Canada." Other achievements of the difficult mission in Kandahar—an improved irrigation system for Panjwayi, better crops undermining drug protection, and an increased role for the ANA and ANP—also generally escaped attention from the Canadian media (Windsor, Charters, and Wilson 2008, 210). The media covered a ramp ceremony on another occasion, as per usual, but missed—from a military point of view—the key part of the story: destruction of a Taliban IED cell near Howz-e-Madad. The full story here would also include the point that the Taliban had been forced to focus on the Canadian battle group and Afghan forces rather than PRT efforts (Windsor, Charters, and Wilson 2008, 193).

Central to all critiques of media coverage is a perceived fixation on casualties and the detainee controversy. Consider these observations from Windsor, Charters, and Wilson (2008, 209–10) about an IED attack and concerns about vehicle safety: "The questions were understandable. But those raising them seemed to have only one measure of mission success or failure: the Canadian body count." Those on the receiving end of such attention also have criticized the media, "who feed like vultures on death, turning other people's suffering into a spectacle or sound bite" (Murray 2011, 204–5; see also Windsor, Charters, and Wilson 2008, xx).

Something of a chicken-and-egg effect may be at work regarding casualties and media coverage. This assessment comes out of an idea-based approach. Antiwar opinion focused on how the military role in Afghanistan departed from the Canadian human security and peacekeeping tradition (Windsor, Charters, and Wilson 2008, 148). An underlying sensitivity to casualties, therefore, could be anticipated to exist among the public. Those in favour of peacekeeping and against war-fighting would quickly point to casualties as an unfortunate side effect of the new policy in place and thus the media would have a built-in audience for its coverage. The very high sensitivity to casualties is brought out by the numbers themselves. Overall Canadian casualties after a decade in Afghanistan reached 157. This is a small fraction of Canadian losses even in individual battles from the two world wars. Yet Stein and Lang (2007, 233) point out that Harper had to deal with controversy over casualties when the total reached eight over the course of his first four months in office. These simple numbers make the point in a compelling way; the self-image of Canada as a peaceful nation, with aversion to loss of life from involvement in war, had not disappeared as a result of the years in Afghanistan.

Why, in sum, did Canada stay the course and even expand its activities in Afghanistan? The Independent Panel (2008, 32) offers a host of reasons:

> Canadian interests and values, and Canadian lives, are now invested in Afghanistan. The sacrifices made there, by Canadians and their families, must be respected. What we do there (or stop doing) affects the Afghan people. It can affect Canadian security. It can affect Canada's reputation in the world. It can affect our influence in international affairs, particularly with respect to future international responses to the dangers and deprivations of failed and fragile states. Canada is a wealthy G8 country; our good fortune and standing impose on us both authority and obligations in global affairs.

Based on that summary, all four of the perspectives—realism, liberalism, the world of ideas, and the government and domestic politics—clearly have played a role in shaping the characteristics of Canadian involvement in Afghanistan. The inertial or momentum-based version of government and domestic politics offers some insight, but it just begins to provide an explanation for the expanding commitment. An idea-based perspective focuses needed attention on the uneasy coexistence of liberal and realist thinking from the escalation of 2005 onward. An active media, which generally favoured a liberal philosophy brought into being through a focus on human security and peacekeeping, played a role in the war of ideas underway at the home front. This conflicted with a Canadian government that increasingly adopted a realist perspective on the events unfolding in Afghanistan.

Consequences: Afghanistan and Canada—Different than Before?

Canada's war in Afghanistan, aside from its training mission, ended at 11:18 a.m. on 7 July 2011. At that time command of remaining CF in Afghanistan shifted to a US officer representing NATO. Canada's military personnel moved on to training activities. It therefore is feasible to begin assessing the legacy of Canadian involvement in Afghanistan at this point for both countries. Of course, from the Government of Canada (Canada 2011a, 13) to virtually any other commentator, a sensible view appreciates that it is very challenging to assess the situation in Afghanistan. While Canada no longer is fighting there, Afghanistan continues to endure insurgency and counter-insurgency. Even more caution, of course, is called for regarding any type of forecasting over the long term. Wartime conditions not only complicate the quest for current information but also put a heavy mist in front of anyone's crystal ball. The following tentative assessment of Afghanistan covers national stability, development and reconstruction, and security. Attention then turns to the legacy for Canada of its decade of involvement in the latest Afghan war.

What about national stability? Afghanistan held another election for the Wolesi Jirga, its lower house of parliament, on 18 September 2010. While accusations of fraud occurred once again, the International Electoral Commission and the Electoral Complaints Commission performed well (Canada 2011a, 2). The regular occurrence of even flawed elections seems likely to have some favourable impact on underlying levels of acceptance for democratic governance.

National stability requires the Afghan government, in a word, to become credible (Horn 2010, 141). Major challenges such as the following continue: the middling state of the ANP, lack of capacity in government institutions, poverty, illiteracy, inadequate water management, lack of security, and lack of UN experience in coordinating a reconstruction effort as large as the one in Afghanistan (Holland 2010, 287; Pigott 2007, 19). Illiteracy, for example, is 72 percent: 57 percent for men and 87 percent for women (Holland 2009, 49). Even by 2007, most Afghans still lived on less than US$1 per day and the country suffered from a negative investment climate (CSPC 2008, 33). All of this is true in spite of Afghanistan receiving more money from the developed world than any other government (Holland 2009, 1).

More encompassing concerns relate to values. Is Afghan traditional culture compatible with Western ideas that accompany military intervention and reconstruction? As of 2010, Afghanistan ranked as the third most corrupt government in the world. While the coalition focuses on coping with corruption and a "culture of impunity," informed observers have asked "How much corruption is acceptable and necessary to lubricate government?" (Chaudhuri and Farrell 2011, 284, 285). The Bonn Agreement's call for an end to corruption seems quite naive in light of such pointed questions a decade later.

Canada's sustained role in Afghan reconstruction and development features three Signature Projects as its intended principal legacies: the Dahla Dam and irrigation system, polio eradication, and education. Carried out by PRTs, these projects follow from the recommendations of the Independent Panel (2008).[2] Through what has become known as a whole of government approach, Canada seeks to achieve the goals specified by the Afghan Compact in its Afghan National Development Strategy: good governance, security, and development (Holland 2009, v).

Rehabilitation of the Dahla Dam and irrigation system, which will entail an investment of up to $50 million, is highly visible and creates the most employment for Afghans among Canadian Signature Projects: "repair of the Dahla Dam and its irrigation system will ensure a secure irrigation water supply to the majority of the Kandahari population, generating 10,000 seasonal jobs and revitalizing the area's once robust agro-economy by providing farmers with irrigated land" (Holland 2010, 282). Kandahar, in fact, quite recently saw its first saffron crop in decades as a result of water provided by the dam (DFAIT 2011e).

Holland (2010, 284–86) offers an authoritative review, based on interviews with leaders, of results from the PRT's wide range of activities in Kandahar:

- enhanced security and mine-risk education;
- support for the National Solidarity Program and the National Area-Base Development Program;
- support for UN-HABITAT;
- improvements to the City of Kandahar's infrastructure and the capacity of its administration;
- economic development, vocational training, and microfinancing;
- rehabilitation of the Dahla Dam and irrigation schemes;
- support for the rule of law and rehabilitation of Sarposa prison;
- construction and rehabilitation of schools and training of Afghan teachers; and
- improved relationships with the Afghan people.

This list conveys Canadian accomplishments in Afghan development broadly construed. It is interesting to pause and consider what kind of change this represents "by the numbers," with the understanding that Canadian efforts account for only part of the improvements observed.

Afghanistan definitely had major progress to its credit in economic terms by 2007: growth averaging 8.7 percent per year, inflation in single digits, a stable Afghani against the dollar, central bank revenues of more than $5 billion, rising agricultural output, a construction boom, massive refugee return, the beginnings of integration into the regional economy, and $3 billion per year in foreign assistance (CSPC 2008, 33, 34).

Table 4-2 provides a comparison between 2001 and 2008 regarding progress in material terms. A range of indicators, from school attendance (micro-level) to electricity produced (macro-level), show improvement by various orders of magnitude. In January 2009, Kabul for the first time had electrical power around the clock. By 2009, the country featured many more health clinics and hospitals and more than 80 percent of Afghans had access to basic health services; in particular, a high percentage of children have been immunized (Holland 2009, ix).

With regard to the security front, tactical operations seem to be going well. ISAF and ANP continue to make progress against the Taliban in both Helmand and Kandahar (Chaudhuri and Farrell 2011, 293; Canada 2011a, 1, 3). However, the situation at a strategic level remains in doubt. Tactical successes, as just described, are not sufficient to overcome "the three strategic obstacles to campaign success: a corrupt and unreliable national government, declining domestic political support for the war in NATO countries, and insurgent safe havens in Pakistan" (Chaudhuri and Farrell 2011, 284, 293). Oddly enough, it can make sense to say that Afghanistan "is getting better and worse at the same time" (Day 2010, 148).

Progress made in the south is readily apparent. While it is too soon to assess the consequences of ISAF's campaign, one concern is that success there simply may displace insurgents to other places in the country

Table 4-2   Afghanistan by the Numbers, 2001 versus 2008

Indicator	2001	2008
Per capita income	US$70	US$300
People with access to telecommunications facilities	15,000	More than 4,000,000
Megawatts of electricity produced	430	754
School attendance	1,000,000 boys, no girls	6,200,000 children, including 2,000,000 girls

Source: Adapted from Holland 2009, ix

(Chaudhuri and Farrell 2011, 283). The related story of the ANA and ANP appears to be a classic case of the half full/half empty glass. Both of these organizations have expanded in size, but informed observers are not able to conclude that quality is significantly higher in either case (Chaudhuri and Farrell 2011, 276; see also Holland 2009, 28). At the same time, a survey question on whether the ANA helps improve security received an 89 percent "yes" response in 2010 (Chaudhuri and Farrell 2011, 277).[3] An improving perception of the ANA may be almost as important as its objective level of performance.

Conversation among the leading governments of the coalition—those who have fought the insurgency with troops rather than rhetoric—is about the endgame. Talk of a 2014 outer limit for involvement in Afghanistan is the norm now in Washington, DC; London; and Ottawa. Public support for an even longer war is very limited. Critics point to the lack of an effective, believable "strategic narrative" on the part of NATO to convince the public at large that sustaining the war effort is worthwhile (Chaudhuri and Farrell 2011, 294). The "political reality" is that NATO troops are virtually certain to leave in 2014 (Chaudhuri and Farrell 2011, 290).

Chaudhuri and Farrell (2011, 295) sum up the current situation as follows:

> the most likely scenario is that operational progress will fail to produce the desired strategic outcomes. Indeed, it is entirely possible that things will get worse on the strategic side of things. Growing war-weariness among NATO publics, a strong and largely immovable patronage system led by corrupt power brokers in Afghanistan, and the strategic logic underlying Pakistani non-action may collectively tip the campaign into a downward spiral.

This summary reinforces an earlier charge made by the *Afghanistan Study Group Report* (CSPC 2008, 11) concerning deficient strategic vision. The problems noted here simply may be endemic to multilateral ventures in pursuit of security.

Even after a decade of effort, challenges facing the coalition continue to be formidable. Kabul's rejection of the Durand Line (a colonial era border demarcation, from 1893), alongside relations with Pakistan in general, continue to pose problems (CSPC 2008, 15, 37; Stein and Lang 2007, 295). Afghan warlords, while not allies of the Taliban, hardly help with stabilization (Pigott 2007, 67). Afghanistan's large and mountainous terrain makes the border with Pakistan especially porous regarding insurgents (Holland 2009, viii–ix). Eight million Afghans are underemployed or unemployed, with two million involved in poppy cultivation or opium production (Holland 2009, 6). More than one-fifth of the population still lacks access to basic services.

Traffic in narcotics—a peculiar but effective alliance between the Taliban and criminal elements—continues to fund the insurgency. The opium trade has become only more lucrative with time (Windsor, Charters, and Wilson 2008, 32). About 90 percent of the world's illegal supply of opium starts out in Afghanistan (Independent Panel 2008, 15). Afghanistan, by one estimate, has more opium cultivation by area than all the coca in Latin America (CSPC 2008, 31).[4] Particularly insidious is the association of elements in the government itself with the drug trade—a certain path to the loss of legitimacy (Stein and Lang 2007, 224, 225). A key concern, therefore, is to develop alternative means of livelihood for Afghans currently cultivating poppies for the opium trade (CSPC 2008, 31, 32). In the absence of such alternatives, "policies of forcible crop destruction only play into the hands of the Taliban" (Smith 2007, 14). One idea for immediate improvement would be to exploit the legitimate medicinal market for poppies; forcible crop destruction simply helps the Taliban by serving as an unintentional recruiting mechanism (Smith 2007, 5–6, 14).

Faced with such problems, the ANA and ANP reveal low capacity; insurgents continue to show an ability to prevent elections and block development projects. ANA soldiers exhibit fatalism and leave things to chance (Day 2010, 214–15), while the ANP is years away from completing its reforms (Holland 2009, 42). This is in spite of ongoing Canadian efforts to train and expand the ANA and ANP, along with health and customs workers (DFAIT 2011e). Problems also persist throughout the justice system (Smith 2007, 20).

Still another danger is psychological; with time, coalition forces may come to be seen as military occupiers (Holland 2009, 43–45). Even the good intentions of the latest intervention, in which Canada is a major participant, are not enough to prevent what might be labelled as an expiry date among even the most sympathetic Afghans. Deeply rooted in the Afghan experience is suspicion regarding intruders. Thus Canadians run the risk of being seen, increasingly, as occupiers in the protracted conflict even after they transition out of a combat role.

Coalition forces also started with a disadvantage in the hearts and minds competition: the Taliban drove the Soviets out, have tribal connections, and almost certainly would remain around in some form after the Canadians and others are gone (Canada 2006b, 32). With time the Taliban's strategy becomes clear: to win at the strategic level by wearing down national support (Day 2010, 255). In a twist of irony, human security constitutes the key issue; "whichever side could provide the greater protection for families and help sustain their simple livelihood would win" (Windsor, Charters, and Wilson, 2008, 88).[5]

Perhaps the most awkward challenge comes from within ISAF itself: caveats by NATO member governments on combat deployment (Pigott 2007, 85, 198; Blatchford 2008, 255, 357; Hillier 2010, 475; Horn 2010, 45, 46; Saideman and Auerswald 2012). Caveats prevent, in particular, use of troops in combat action. Possible reasons for the persistence of these restrictions include fear of losing, not wanting association with a US-led operation, fear of upsetting Muslims in their own countries, aversion to casualties, or all of the preceding (Smith 2007, 6). Among various others, the *Afghanistan Study Group Report* (CSPC 2008, 17) called for an end to national caveats, citing success in Kosovo in the absence of such restrictions.[6] Given the issue of fatigue among governments raised a moment ago, such a change seems very unlikely. Moreover, the persistence of caveats creates resentment among fully contributing coalition members (such as Canada, during its years of combat activity) and almost certainly affects their likely persistence in a military role.

Afghanistan, to sum up, continues to be in a state of flux. Life for Afghans is both more unstable than it was under the Taliban yet improving in any number of ways. Canada's impact in the short term looks positive in the sense that it combined with other ISAF members to create an opportunity for further nation building. In the long term, however, the fate of Afghanistan remains uncertain. While a return to power for the Taliban seems unlikely, persistent problems in both security and development caution against a prediction of ultimate success.

What about the legacy of the war for Canada? Points of interest include the CF, Canada's role in institutions, lessons learned for development assistance, the direction and level of activity for foreign policy, and Canadian identity.

Afghanistan ended up as the longest war in Canadian history, with more personnel than any other conflict since World War II (Granatstein and Oliver 2011, 3, 4). Canada's experience in Afghanistan altered public views of its military (Windsor, Charters, and Wilson 2008, 57). Evidence of changing attitudes is easy to find in both opinion data and through anecdotes. For example, passengers on a flight to Edmonton learned of returning Canadian military on board and "burst into spontaneous applause and prolonged cheers" (Blatchford 2008, 319). Some see a restoration of pride in the CF, as indicated by an increased interest in the Canadian War Museum (Granatstein and Oliver 2011, 8). General Hillier (2010, 492) puts this very emphatically: for the first time since World War II, Canadians saw the CF as "*their* armed forces." This represented quite a change from the 1990s, when military personnel had been told and even ordered not to wear their uniforms in public (Blatchford 2008, 320).

Canada's Afghan odyssey also affected the self-image of the CF as an entity. The war, from the standpoint of one observer, "transformed the capacity and purpose of our military" (Owen 2010). General Hillier (2010, 494) observes that "immense frustration at the ignorance of so many who labeled us 'only' peacekeepers had disappeared." Major Bill Fletcher asserted that the reputation of the Canadian military had improved "on the world stage" (quoted in Wattie 2008, 293). One observer goes as far as to pronounce the "national peacekeeper myth" as "dead" (Horn 2010, 147). Obviously Canadians might vary as to whether these developments are good or bad, but no one could deny that the CF had changed and possibly in a sustained way.

Points of continuity in the Canadian mindset regarding human security, however, also can be found in even the "new" CF. Murray (2011, 113) asserts that Canadian soldiers look for social value in what they do and their words back her up. The text box "Canadian Soldiers on Why We Fight" depicts examples of commonly expressed sentiments from members of the CF conveyed in accounts of their activities on the ground. The

Canadian Soldiers on Why We Fight

"These kids want to go to school. . . . I think that's where Canadians do rise above most of the other nations that are over there, we're fighting on a multi-level system. We're not saving Afghanistan so that we can do free trade with them after; I mean, you can import rugs to Canada, but it's not an industrial country." —Corporal Ashley Van Leeuwen (quoted in Blatchford 2008, 62)

"No one else was willing to take those types of risk to be able to support the Afghan government like we did." —Major Kirk Gallinger (quoted in Blatchford 2008, 229)

"Take the time to challenge anyone who attempts to diminish what you did. Don't get mad, but take the time." —Lieutenant Colonel Ian Hope (quoted in Blatchford 2008, 317)

"These people need help. Do you know what the Taliban are doing to women? Imprisoning them in their homes and underneath those burkas. They're bartered and sold like pieces of property. And children aren't allowed to go to school. The Taliban burn down the schools and kill the teachers." —Captain Jeff Francis (quoted in Murray 2011, 141, 165)

"[W]hen we leave, the Taliban slide in at night and force them to cough up food and stuff. And also, the Taliban are running around calling themselves mujahedeen, so they look like they are fighting occupiers." —Warrant Officer Jim Murnaghan (quoted in Day 2010, 166)

comments illustrate the persistence of human security in the mindset of the CF. Canadian soldiers want to feel positive about their impact. This is not experienced in terms of satisfaction from military conquest but instead the ability to facilitate a better way of life by protecting people from danger. While their combat actions reflect realism, motivations expressed by members of the CF reserve a place for liberalism as well.

Canada's role in NATO, along with the organization itself, will not be the same after the years spent in Afghanistan. Even as early as 2007, observers began to wonder about the viability of NATO (Stein and Lang 2007, 292). With time, critics went much further than that assessment; Afghanistan, at least to some, had "demonstrated the serious operational deficiencies of the efforts led by both NATO and the UN" (Owen 2010). General Hillier (2010, 477) sees success in Afghanistan as vital to the survival of NATO. Yet the behaviour of some of its allies must give pause to a Canada that came through with a full effort in Afghanistan. Certainly a period of reflection is needed on the future commitment of resources to NATO in particular, with further difficulties in Libya (see Chapter 6) simply reflecting that point.

What about the development and reconstruction side of the Canadian decade in Afghanistan? As a result of the Afghan experience, the Canadian government is more aware of serious problems regarding the provision of aid. These difficulties have implications for programs beyond Afghanistan. Problems ensued there because development assistance, such as that provided by CIDA, goes through national programs. This is especially bad in Afghanistan because of its corrupt central government. A key recommendation of multiple government reports, therefore, is to decentralize aid; in particular, Canada's principal military operations had been in Kandahar and thus aid should have been provided directly there as well (Canada 2006b, 28, 29, 30; Independent Panel 2008, 25, 26). Given the high levels of corruption that plague governments throughout the developing world, a decentralized approach should be pursued whenever possible.

What will be Canada's direction and likely degree of foreign policy activity in the world after Afghanistan? One possibility is a new era of isolationism (Dey 2011, 2). After a decade of major investment in human and material terms, there is no victory to declare in Afghanistan. Instead, the fight goes on, with Canada now in the role of military advisor and ongoing contributor to reconstruction. Coupled with an uncertain outcome to the Afghan conflict, the massive investment could discourage further activity abroad for the foreseeable future, especially anything with a military component. This argument comes jointly out of perspectives based on realism and the government and domestic politics. From a realist point of view, the question to ask is this one: Did the war serve Canada's interests in terms of greater security? With anything but an obvious answer available, the focus turns to the impact of military deployment on the standing of politicians. Battle fatigue was apparent with time. From the outlook of a sitting politician, therefore, a case can be made regarding aversion to an active security policy because of known domestic political risks and unknown payoffs, at least based on the recent experience with Afghanistan.

Did Afghanistan bring an end to the liberal mindset in Canadian foreign policy, with its emphasis on cooperation through international institutions and the goal of human security? One possibility is that the war went on long enough to eliminate this philosophy as the one underlying Canadian foreign policy (Dey 2011, 2). Canada, from an idea-oriented point of view, changed its identity as a result of the Afghan experience; it internalized international discourse that focused on national security and also "restored its identity as a military unit" (Dey 2011, 59; see also Fitzsimmons 2009). The story of Canada and Afghanistan tempers any disposition to rely strictly on government and domestic politics for an explanation of foreign policy orientation: "what other states do and say affects a state's national interest as much as the preference of its constituencies" (Dey 2011, 4). Canada's effort to keep up its place among leading countries reflects a realist concept of national interest that had been out of favour for some time.

Perhaps a pendulum metaphor will turn out to be best in assessing the impact of the Afghan war on Canadian identity. Consider these observations on Canadian foreign policy from a long-term perspective (Granatstein and Oliver 2011, 7):

> Contrary to the stubbornly persistent view, especially evident in the deeply anti-military quarters of the political left, that the war had eroded a proud, peacekeeping tradition and decades worth of Canadian foreign policy neutrality, it was completely in keeping with previous overseas commitments and past articulations of Canadian interests.

From that standpoint, the war represented a *return* to an earlier profile in Canadian security policy—what might be viewed as a pendulum swinging back to something like a centre position.

As opposed to peacekeeping, which had reigned supreme in ideology if not commitment of resources for decades, consider the mythology associated with Vimy Ridge. Canadian troops fought under their own command for the first time in that horrendous battle from World War I. This victory from 1917 became a "key marker in the development of Canadian nationalism" (Granatstein and Oliver 2011, 437; see also Windsor, Charters, and Wilson 2008, xvii–xviii; Hillier 2010, 157). Ironic, too, is that it contained a mythological element; military historians, in spite of whatever Canadians themselves might have wanted to think, saw little impact of this battle on the successful outcome of the war (Granatstein and Oliver 2011, 439). Instead, the approximately 3,600 Canadians who died in the battle played a limited part in an international trauma that claimed millions of lives. As with peacekeeping, the myth-making of Vimy Ridge involves exaggeration—not on the part of those who served with great honour in the military, but instead among others who built up Vimy Ridge into a decisive battle. The ascent of Vimy Ridge into mythology parallels the later tendency to exaggerate the Canadian role in peacekeeping, which certainly had atrophied to a considerable degree by the time of the Afghan war.[7]

Colourful as ever, General Hillier (2010, 430) lends credence to the idea of a swinging pendulum as something that can represent Canadian identity over the course of decades: "for so many years, our political landscape has been dominated by a select group in Canadian society, self-proclaimed opinion leaders who I prefer to think of as snake-oil salesmen, who had been allowed to create the impression that Canadians were very sensitive, would only advocate 'soft power' and would support their military only in the role of peacekeepers." Even those who opposed the Afghan war still had to confront the limits on what could be accomplished without military capability. Their reflections provide insight into the fragility of the liberal peacekeeping mindset, which proved vulnerable to the new challenge represented by the realist experience of Afghanistan. As an example, consider the views of Melanie Murray, author of *For Your Tomorrow*, a recollection of her nephew, Jeff Francis, who lost his life in Afghanistan: "As a pacifist, I had never been able to resolve the problem of how to combat the evil that exists in the world. What do you do when the barbarians are at the gate? What would I do if the lives of my own children were threatened? Speak softly and carry a big stick?" (2011, 111).

Perhaps Afghanistan altered Canadian identity precisely because the pendulum had swung so far in one direction that it became easily prone to reversal. Afghanistan challenged moral relativism in particular. Consider this imagined reflection on the part of a Canadian soldier who formerly had been working on a doctorate at a major Canadian university: "He thinks about academics with their 'cultural relativism' rhetoric, claiming that all social beliefs and customs are equally valid and dependent on the cultural environment. Beam them down from their ivory towers, he thinks, to walk a mile across the scorching sand in a burka" (Murray 2011, 156). Moral absolutism is inherent in that passage; some things are just wrong after all. Such views are more in tune with the use of force, on the one hand. Promotion of human security, on the other hand, also can be in line with military action of the kind pursued by Canada in Afghanistan. As opposed to conquest, a clear consciousness exists regarding a fight for Afghanistan's future as one that will include human rights and democracy (Murray 2011, 229, 234). Thus realist *means* sometimes may prove essential to liberal *ends*.

Consider the reactions of Canadian soldiers in general to conditions in Afghanistan. Their views point toward a pendulum that had moved back to the centre: "For Canadian soldiers trained in the laws of armed combat, the deliberate targeting of civilians was more than just unlawful; it was evil. To the India Company troops, maiming a child was certainly a strange way for the Taliban to convince Afghans that they deserved to rule" (Windsor, Charters, and Wilson 2008, 90). One embedded observer makes a further, specific assessment of the CF's reactions to what they saw while deployed: "To see the hardened Patricia paratroopers on watch at Sperwan Ghar, the shouts to happy children in the cool evening convinced many of the importance of their task" (Windsor, Charters, and Wilson 2008, 115). This hardly sounds out of line with a commitment to human security even in the midst of fighting a war.

Afghanistan, in sum, looks like the force that pulled the Canadian identity pendulum back to a centre position. The previously ascendant peacekeeping image "was not only deeply ingrained in the public, but it was also wildly popular. That it did not fit well with Canada's history did not much matter to the public" (Stein and Lang 2007, 19). An exclusive focus on peacekeeping among successive governments and media flew in the face of Canadian history. Canada had played highly conventional and effective military roles throughout the twentieth century, with World Wars I and II, and the Korean War, as prime examples. Human security and peacekeeping represented significant departures from long-standing traditions within Canadian foreign policy, which had included overseas combat in pursuit of perceived national interests. Perhaps, after the Afghan war, Canada is back in a more sustainable position, with its pendulum of identity balanced between liberal and realist forces, essential to self-esteem in the one direction and national security in the other.

Reflections on Canada and Afghanistan

Canada went to Afghanistan on a quest for change. The jury remains out on what will happen to Afghanistan after the Western intervention someday comes to an end. The impact of Canadian efforts on both security and development as part of the ISAF team is apparent. Previously dangerous places are safer than before, but the risk of insurgency returning to any given location is never very far away. Development indicators are up across the board, but whether progress in the form of Canadian Signature Projects and other more limited activities can be sustained is open to question.

Ironic, then, is that the more certain change to come out of the decade in Afghanistan concerns Canada itself. As the first sustained combat experience for Canada in about half a century, the Afghan war's short-term impact concerns both security policy on the surface and the deeper matter of national identity. Canadians rediscovered that they could fight a war and had mixed feelings about it; the military performed extremely well but loss of life from combat action had been a nearly forgotten aspect of this type of activity. As for identity, it is impossible to say whether the momentum will be sustained, but the pendulum swung away from liberal sensibilities regarding human security and toward a realist emphasis on government security through pursuit of national interests. The chapters that follow will turn to Canada's security-related experience with its neighbour and principal ally, the United States, in the years leading up to 9/11 and beyond.

Chapter 5

The Elephant and the Muskox: Canada–US Relations

How and Why?

Ottawa's connection with Washington, or Can/Am relations, provides the focus for this chapter and the next. This chapter considers context and causes, and the next examines characteristics and consequences regarding security relations over the last decade. As with the study of Afghanistan in Chapters 2, 3, and 4, assessment of Can/Am security relations is guided by perspectives such as realism, liberalism, the world of ideas, and the government and domestic politics.

The main focus here on this vast topic will be primarily on the realm of Can/Am security.[1] (Even seemingly opposite cases, in and outside of the security realm, will have aspects that overlap. For example, the Canadian decision to stay out of the Iraq War had possible economic implications; the US might decide to reward or punish its allies based on their degree of support for the venture. Another instance would be the Kyoto Protocol on the environment; economic burdens imposed by honouring such an agreement could reduce resources available for military purposes.) Here we will consider a standard, national defence-centred definition of security.[2]

Key topics are border management, the Arctic, BMD, the Iraq War, and Libyan intervention. All of these matters also have attracted a qualitatively higher level of attention from both practitioners and scholars than other Can/Am security issues, with one exception (e.g., Potter 2008, 150).[3]

I will discuss this topic in a generally chronological way. Overlap in issues suggests the value of an account that blends events together into a single narrative, as with security and development in the preceding chapters on Afghanistan. The review starts with Can/Am relations at a general level, with specific issues arising along the way. Some issues, such as border security and the Arctic, are long-standing. Others, such as BMD and especially Iraq and Libya, have much more recent origins.

Context: Who Is in the Zoo and What Do They Do?

Former prime minister Pierre Trudeau famously compared Canada to a mouse sitting next to a US elephant. Interesting to ponder is that the local zoo may be a bit different than the extreme pairing just noted: On the one hand, the US is not just Canada's elephant but compares to the rest of the world in about the same way. Its military prowess in particular is immense even in comparison to states such as the increasingly prominent BRIC: Brazil, Russia, India, and China. On the other hand, Canada is not a mouse but more like a "smallish hippo, a buffalo, or muskox" that experiences but also shapes the policies of its elephantine neighbour (Dyment 2010, 50). Canada is about 10 percent of the US in terms of population and size of economy; its land mass is even larger than that of the southern neighbour. Canada's natural resource endowment rivals any country in the world. A less extreme comparison—elephant and buffalo, for example—might seem more in order, given the many factors beyond military power.

Regardless of what animals are taken to reside in this particular zoo, it is clear that the relationship they have with each other is by far the most important for one of those concerned. Relations with the US tower above all others for Canada in terms of both importance and difficulty (Bercuson 2005, 8; Bercuson and Stairs 2005, 3; Fergusson 2005b, 62; Potter 2008, 148). Given the disparity of size, Canada attends to the US and is affected by it much more than the reverse. Look at it this way: while Canada's interactions with the rest of the world can be based on preference, its relationship with the US is driven by necessity and may be "electorally inconvenient" (Bercuson and Stairs 2005, 4). In other words, policy in the national interest must be tempered, given public sensibilities, by maintaining a degree of distance from the US. Thus Canadian governments are fated to an inherently difficult balancing act. While Canadians want the prime minister to stand up to the president, generally speaking, that can be unwise.

For the US, Canada is a border state, long-standing ally, and major trading partner. So Ottawa is not without significance to Washington. An inherent asymmetry of interest, however, persists. As world system leader, the US must attend to the security of all regions. Moreover, its economic linkages are not so concentrated in Canada as the reverse. Canada is significant to the US but largely out of daily consciousness.

Hundreds of years of interactions characterize the two countries' relationship. This chapter reviews major historical figures and events in the security domain (Bothwell 2006).

Consider border management. Given their long-standing and close friendship, it is interesting to find that conflict rather than cooperation more accurately describes relations between Canada and the US over the course of previous centuries. Defence relations with the US stretch well back before Confederation and even the American Revolution. Prior to the Declaration of Independence in 1776, an invading army came from the seaboard colonies to Montreal and Quebec (Thompson and Randall 2008, 333; Granatstein and Oliver 2011, 73). United Empire Loyalists, who fled the newly independent United States, formed a significant settlement group in Canada. With the onset of the War of 1812, the US most prominently tried to take over the remaining British colonies north of its border. Washington's lacklustre effort in that conflict produced a draw with its British adversary. In the aftermath of the war, border tensions continued during the nineteenth century. The US offered modest assistance to Canadian rebels in 1837 and the Confederacy launched attacks from Canada on the Union during the Civil War. Intrusions from Fenian raiders based in New England took place in the Maritimes after the war's conclusion (Granatstein and Oliver 2011, 73; see also Bothwell 2006; Thompson and Randall 2008, 333).[4] It would be fair to say that border management, through the end of the nineteenth century, reflected an uneasy compromise over boundaries rather than active cooperation.

The Arctic is like the border itself, and remains a matter of long-standing concern. Consider some basic geographic facts: 40 percent of the Canadian land mass and 162,000 kilometres of coastline are in the Arctic (Canada 2011b). Conflict over the vast Arctic is an offshoot of border tensions that have already been in place for a long time. Canadians generally live within 150 kilometres or so of the US border given its temperate climate in comparison to the north, especially the Arctic. For most Canadians, historically speaking, the north "remained as a land of untested promise and potential" (Nord 2006, 291, 292). Prime Minister Harper put the somewhat eccentric combination of distance and attachment regarding the Arctic in this way during a speech from 10 August 2007: "Even Canadians who have never been north of 60 [degrees latitude] feel it" (Canada 2007).

Tensions with the US oscillated throughout the nineteenth century. As a residual effect of Britain's tacit support for the Confederacy during the Civil War, the reunified and increasingly powerful US "twisted the lion's tail" when given the opportunity. The US acquired Alaska from the Russian Empire at the time of Confederation and thus created a second border with Canada, which still conducted foreign policy under British authority until decades later. The matter of Arctic sovereignty, however, came under Canadian jurisdiction in 1880 and caused "anxiety" in Ottawa ever since (Lajeunesse 2007–8, 75). Bickering over what now is known as the Alaska Panhandle continued in the late nineteenth century as British and US power waned and waxed, respectively, in North America. Thus Arctic sovereignty and the border became intertwined as security issues for the US and Canada a long time ago.

Tensions subsided after settlement of the Alaska boundary dispute through arbitration in 1903. (Some degree of Canadian dissatisfaction and anxiety lingered for years afterwards [Nord 2006, 292].) This agreement also signalled the beginning of the end for Canadian foreign relations conducted under the auspices of the British Empire. In fact, it became possible for the first time to "speak of Canadian-American relations of an intergovernmental kind" (Bothwell 2006, 272). From the governments of Wilfrid Laurier and Theodore Roosevelt onward, the twentieth century saw Canada and the US develop and maintain one of the most trusting and effective alliances in the world. Security-related institutions accumulated and, importantly, no longer involved British participation in setting things up. For example, the successful Boundary Waters Treaty of 1909 created an International Joint Commission that exists to this day (Bothwell 2006, 274). Border management transitioned into an issue that focused on *mutual* security in relation to potential third-party threats as opposed to a point of conflict between the neighbours themselves.

Disagreement with the US over Arctic sovereignty, in spite of many other accumulating mutual interests, occurred sporadically throughout the twentieth century and continues to this day. Canada traditionally put forward the sector principle in making its case. The sector principle holds that control over territory extends north from a given land mass, in the shape of a pie wedge, until reaching the pole. This concept is highly favourable to Canada because of its array of islands in the Far North. (The principle's first articulation goes back to a speech by Pascal Poirier in the Canadian Senate in 1907 [Parker and Madjd-Sadjadi 2010, 341].) It almost goes without saying that the sector theory is not well-received outside of Canada, with the US as a long-standing critic of Canadian claims.

Although in principle it could do so because of Alaska, the US does not make a land-based claim.[5] Instead, the US Arctic agenda for a very long time has been about access to waterways. Notable in particular would be an ability to use the Northwest Passage, "usually defined as the body of Arctic water existing between the Davis Strait and Baffin Bay in the east and the Bering Strait in the west" (Carnaghan and Goody 2006, 2). The US has argued consistently that "the Northwest Passage represents an international strait (international waters), which allows the right of transit passage (beyond 'innocent passage')" (Carnaghan and Goody 2006, 3). Interest in the Arctic built in the US, for instance, as a result of significantly more successful exploration during the early twentieth century. The Norwegian Roald Amundsen managed to traverse the Northwest Passage as early as 1909. Observers at the time understood the significance of this route as a potential path to Asia. The difficulty of the journey, along with opening of the Panama Canal in 1914, put the issue of Arctic access on the back burner for the US (Parker and Madjd-Sadjadi 2010, 337).

Security cooperation between the US and Canada became even closer as the twentieth century progressed. The two neighbours successfully fought as allies in World War I. During the Depression, dictators in Europe and Asia menaced the democratic world and many could see war coming. This became more clear as the 1930s moved forward. On 18 August 1938, President Franklin D. Roosevelt offered Canada a security guarantee. Two days later, Prime Minister Mackenzie King stated that Canada would not allow enemy forces to enter the US through Canada (Clarkson 2002, 382).[6] These exchanges culminated in the Ogdensberg Declaration, which in August 1940 "voiced the concept of joint defense and sanctioned the establishment of the Canada-U.S. (CANUS) Permanent Joint Board on Defense" (Renuart 2009, 93). Then, as might have been expected, Canada and the US fought together once again victoriously as allies in World War II.

Security cooperation picked up after the war. Canada signed the NATO treaty on 1 April 1949. The US and Canada built military bases and stationed troops in the north (Nord 2007, 210). Canada also joined the US-led coalition that, under the UN banner, fought the North Koreans and Chinese to a standstill on the Korean peninsula from 1950 to 1953 (Stairs 1974; Bothwell 2006, 376–79; Nord 2007, 2010). All of these actions reflected ongoing concerns about potential Soviet aggression against the Western democracies.

Canada and the US established NORAD on 12 May 1958.[7] A product of the Cold War, NORAD came into being as an institutional response to the security risk of Soviet long-range bombers and later missiles that might come over the pole. (Potential attacks from east and west already could be detected through air and naval patrols.) NORAD provides air and space warning and defends aerospace sovereignty for the two partner states. (For Canada in particular, NORAD provides access to new technology and vast amounts of information from the US.) Peterson Air Force Base in Colorado Springs is the headquarters for NORAD, while joint command and control is nearby at the Cheyenne Mountain Directorate of the Cheyenne Mountain Air Force Station. At the Canadian Forces Base (CFB) in North Bay, Ontario, NORAD maintains a command and control centre as well. Headquarters for Canada as one of the three NORAD regions (the others are the continental US and Alaska) are maintained at CFB Winnipeg, where the 1 Canadian Air Division is responsible for protection of Canadian aerospace.

NORAD effectively integrated a series of earlier steps designed to meet the need for warning against Soviet attack by air over the polar region. Canada and the US opened radar stations, which increased in quantity and quality during the Cold War, in an effort to improve warning time. This process started with the Pinetree Radar Defence System in 1951 (Nord 2006, 294; see also Nord 2007, 210). The Distant Early Warning (DEW) Line, completed in 1957, provided the best coverage yet of the Far North. The DEW Line included 58 monitoring stations. With such extensive dual arrangements in place, it made sense to coordinate activities—hence NORAD. The degree of integration in place so long ago created an inertial effect; if one ally put forward a new initiative in continental security, the other naturally would become involved through existing institutions.

Events on the other side of the world, meanwhile, would reverberate in later Canadian involvement with Libya.[8] In a superficial way, Libya resembles Canada in its geostrategic placement. Libya is next door to a vastly more populated and powerful state, namely, Egypt (St. John 2011, 113). In terms of government and foreign policy, however, it hardly could be more different than Canada. Until the very recent overthrow of its dictatorship, Libya had no experience with democracy and resided far outside of the normal Canadian peer group. On 1 September 1969, Captain (later Colonel) Moammar al Gadhafi overthrew the Libyan monarchy and set in motion a new set of policies. His Revolutionary Command Council (RCC), modelled on Gamal Nasser's executive council of military officers in Egypt, with the same name, did not bring about anything that resembled a shift toward democracy. Instead, led by Gadhafi, the RCC banned independent political parties. The new regime's intense new rhetoric denounced imperialism and Zionism. While it had tensions with Islamists, the RCC claimed to be both Arab nationalist and jihadist. In essence, the RCC practised a unique form of socialism, combined with a combative attitude that led quickly to support, at least in words, for international terrorism. The final point, on two later occasions, would stimulate Canadian involvement with this distant and troubled state.

Back in North America, cooperation mixed with conflict in the Arctic for Canada and the US as the Cold War continued. Then as now, Canada defends its claim to the Far North on the basis of "use and occupancy" (quoted in Carnaghan and Goody 2006, 2). Canadian sensitivity regarding Arctic sovereignty heightened as a result of the voyage made by the SS *Manhattan* in the fall of 1969. Owned by Humble Oil, this icebreaking tanker started out from Philadelphia with the goal of going through the Northwest Passage to Alaska. Oil had been discovered at Prudhoe Bay (Parker and Madjd-Sadjadi 2010, 336). The company wanted to assess the economic feasibility of using vessels like the *Manhattan* to bring oil from Alaska to the lower 48 states. The *Manhattan* broke through most obstacles easily but did need assistance at times from the icebreakers *Westwind* and *Northwind* (US Coast Guard) and *John A. Macdonald* (Canadian Navy). When it reached Prudhoe Bay on the north shore of Alaska, the *Manhattan* "took on a ceremonial barrel of oil" (Kavanagh 2005). While the ship successfully came back through the Northwest Passage (and made one other trip), data from its journey suggested that moving oil from Alaska overland would be more economical—hence the building of the Trans-Alaska Pipeline soon after.

Over and beyond escorting the tanker with an icebreaker, Canada reacted immediately to the *Manhattan* as a challenge to sovereignty. With the voyage still in progress, legislators "brought pressure on the government to declare the Northwest Passage Canadian territorial waters" ("The Manhattan's Epic Voyage" 1969). Trudeau responded with the Arctic Waters Pollution Prevention Act. This Act cited the need to prevent pollution as the basis for an effort to extend Canadian jurisdiction out to 160 kilometres beyond the coast (Parker and Madjd-Sadjadi 2010, 343).

Arctic tensions foreshadowed a major shift in Can/Am relations. Canada moved in a nationalist direction and pursued distance from the United States with the announcement of Trudeau's Third Option policy at the outset of the 1970s. This initiative argued that Canada should move away from its close connection with the US, just as it had obtained separation from Great Britain at an earlier stage of history. The nationalist coalition in Canadian politics, led by Trudeau, had come to believe that, without significant countermeasures in areas such as energy and investment, Canada would drift closer to the US. Such inertia would pose a great risk to Canadian sovereignty. In conjunction with the National Energy Program and the Foreign Investment Review Agency as specific policies driven by economic nationalism, articulation of the Third Option looked unfriendly to the US in particular. From the standpoint of Trudeau and his supporters, the Third Option put into words a quest for independence from the US (Gotlieb 2004, 17; Barry 2007, 118). The policy, which looked beyond traditional Canadian partners, seemed to be about finding "new and presumably better friends" (Sands 2011, 1). At one point, Trudeau even talked about leaving NATO.

Once again events on the other side of the world are inserted into the story of Can/Am security relations. On 16 July 1979, Saddam Hussein—the most powerful figure in Iraq, de facto, since 1968—forced his ailing predecessor from power and became president of Iraq. He imposed one of the most brutal dictatorships in history from that point onward. Saddam went to war against Iran in 1980. His later efforts at conquest would end up requiring Canada to decide whether to participate in respective US-led, multilateral interventions against Iraq.

Canada's tensions with the US increased and peaked when the conservative Republican Ronald Reagan became president in 1981. Reagan-era policy statements from the US put a new emphasis on defence issues in the Arctic (Nord 2006, 295–96). Cruise missile testing in the Canadian north, proposed by Reagan, marks an approximate beginning to the context of BMD as a Can/Am security issue.

Testing ultimately occurred after Trudeau gave in to "extreme pressure" from the US (Bercuson 2005, 7). Trudeau (quoted in Lennox 2009, 66) observed at the time that "it is hardly fair to rely on the Americans to protect the West, but [to] refuse to lend them a hand when the going gets rough." The prime minister faced cross-pressure from his domestic constituency—a centre-left coalition that tended to be anti-American and skeptical about the military—and the need to stay on board with Washington as the principal alliance partner. The latter concern became pre-eminent as the renewed Cold War reached its height. Perhaps the peace mission of the prime minister, which involved travelling to world capitals toward the end of his time in office, along with saying "yes" to at least one form of missile defence, reflected the ongoing existence of such cross-pressures at varying levels.

BMD came to the forefront with the Reagan administration's invitation to Canada in 1983 to join the Strategic Defence Initiative (SDI). According to former prime minister Paul Martin (2008, 384), the origins of the US BMD program lie in this Reagan-era initiative. Controversy quickly ensued as it became clear that SDI moved the US away from and possibly violated the testing ban in the Anti-ballistic Missile Treaty that had been signed by the superpowers in 1972. Labelled derisively by critics as Star Wars, SDI focused on defence against a missile attack. SDI represented a significant departure from the doctrine of mutually assured destruction that had been in place for decades. Instead of counting on the certainty of mutual annihilation to deter an attack, the US and its allies would seek to repel missiles from the USSR in the first place. Prime Minister Brian Mulroney, who had replaced Trudeau in 1984, put forward Canada's response the next year: while no official government involvement would occur, Canadian companies would be permitted to take part in research (Lennox 2009, 73).

While Canada rejected the offer to coordinate on BMD via SDI in an official capacity, the issue did not go away. In the context of NORAD, US efforts toward BMD raised questions about the ability of the two partners to operate their aerospace defence together. Canadian leaders would experience an ongoing dilemma: "how to say yes to information without giving the United States and domestic opinion the perception of saying yes to participation" (Fergusson 2010, 207). More than any other issue, BMD lives up to the metaphor offered earlier about threading the needle between cooperation with the US and keeping some distance for the sake of placating Canadian public opinion.

Replacement of Trudeau with the relatively pro-American Mulroney in 1984 (after a brief interregnum with the Liberal, John Turner, as prime minister) did not end disagreement in the Far North even as cooperation occurred in any number of other areas. For example, within a year, Mulroney eliminated the Foreign Investment Review Agency, National Energy Program, and the Third Option, all of which had been unpopular in Washington. He supported SDI, along with the invasions of Panama (1989) and Kuwait (1991) (Clarkson 2002, 386, 387). At the same time, NORAD evolved in response to technological change; the North Warning System came in as a replacement for the DEW Line from the mid-1980s onward.

Public concern over Arctic sovereignty continued to build in Canada during the early 1980s and, in spite of general cooperation with Washington across a range of other areas, anxiety focused on the US. Skeptical attitudes about the US among the public, reinforced by the media, constrained Mulroney on what to do about Arctic sovereignty in particular. Oil and gas discoveries, along with ongoing US refusal to recognize Canadian sovereignty over the Northwest Passage, created pressure on Ottawa to act on the issue (Lajeunesse 2007–8, 74, 76).

Tensions increased when the US Coast Guard icebreaker, *Polar Sea*, transited the Northwest Passage in 1985 (Lackenbauer and Farish 2007, 937; Parker and Madjd-Sadjadi 2010, 339). The US took the position that it had the right to go from Greenland to Alaska without asking Canadian permission. Washington claimed that it merely had to *notify* Ottawa of such actions in the Far North. While the Canadian government disagreed, the two sides worked out a compromise: the *Polar Sea* would make its voyage, but with Canadian observers aboard the ship.

Tensions continued in Parliament and, near Melville Island, activists dropped leaflets onto the *Polar Sea*.

Given the intensity of public reaction to the latest US incursion in the Arctic, the Mulroney government issued an order in council on 10 September 1985. Canada now explicitly claimed straight baselines around its territory. This meant that the Northwest Passage would be regarded by Canada as an internal waterway. In addition, the Tory government made a commitment to enforce the Arctic Waters Pollution Prevention Act—the Trudeau-era legislation that had been somewhat forgotten by the middle of the 1980s.[9] The Act specifically defined Arctic waters:

> the internal waters of Canada and the waters of the territorial sea of Canada and the exclusive economic zone of Canada, within the area enclosed by the 60th parallel of north latitude, the 141st meridian of west longitude and the outer limit of the exclusive zone; however, where the international boundary between Canada and Greenland is less than 200 nautical miles from the baselines of the territorial sea of Canada, the international boundary shall be substituted for that outer limit.

In addition to this general claim, the Act also contained provisions regarding deposit of waste, civil liability, recovery of claims, enforcement, and punishment. In an overall sense the Act—a highly public restatement of the Trudeau-era legislation on the Arctic—intended to serve as a warning to the US in particular about the consequences of persistent violation of Canadian sovereignty.

Libya comes back into the Can/Am picture briefly in 1986. For years Gadhafi had sponsored terrorism as a way of extending his influence beyond a relatively limited power base (St. John 2011, 125). The Reagan administration imposed sanctions against Libya and then held Gadhafi responsible for a bombing in West Berlin during the spring. In retaliation, the US bombed what it claimed to be "centers of terrorist activity and training" in Tripoli and Benghazi (St. John 2011, 127). Prime Minister Mulroney condemned Libyan support for terrorism and strongly endorsed the US bombing raid. This seemingly isolated series of events foreshadowed greater Canadian involvement in Libya at a later date.

Pressure on the Canadian government to do something about the American presence in the Arctic did not go away, even with sustained and visible cooperation on other security matters such as Libya. Ongoing Canadian concerns about Arctic sovereignty and security explain, at least in part, the 1987 White Paper on Defence. It called for the purchase of submarines that could transit the Northwest Passage in two weeks. The White Paper's policy initiatives, unsurprisingly, received explicit justification in terms of a perceived mounting threat from the USSR (Richter 2006, 59–60; Kite and Nord 2007, 261).

Public opinion drove negotiations with the US that culminated in the Agreement on Arctic Cooperation. Signed in 1988, the Agreement assured Canada that "US icebreakers will obtain transit consent and obey Canadian laws while in Canadian waters" and, in return, guaranteed that "consent will be given for purposes of transit" (Parker and Madjd-Sadjadi 2010, 339). The Agreement thereby resolved one aspect of the issue, but Arctic sovereignty would reappear on the agenda of Can/Am security in short order.

While the Mulroney government responded positively to public worries about US intrusions—notable, given otherwise very friendly relations with Washington—the White Paper ultimately failed to be implemented. The plan for submarines ran aground on shifting public views; with the Cold War coming to an end and financial problems confronting the government, the electorate no longer had enthusiasm for such a major spending initiative on defence (Lajeunesse 2007–8, 80–81; see also Richter 2006, 59–60; Kite and Nord 2007, 261).

During the early 1990s, tensions once again developed with the US, this time over the Canadian-inspired Arctic Council (Nord 2006, 300–1). Ottawa had envisioned the Arctic Council as a clearing house for a comprehensive set of issues among the circumpolar countries. The US, ever mindful of security concerns, saw this potential body in much more limited terms. Washington viewed the Arctic Council as a limited forum for problem solving—and with no anticipated role in defence and issues of military security. Debate over the Arctic Council's mandate dragged on for years.

Developments on the other side of the globe brought the issue of BMD back into play for US defence planners. Iraq invaded and occupied Kuwait in August 1990. When Iraq fired missiles into Saudi Arabia and Israel during the subsequent Gulf War of early 1991, NORAD's state-of-the-art network of sensors alerted the US Central Command. This allowed coalition troops and civilians to be warned about the assaults and also gave time for Patriot missiles to be fired in order to bring down the Iraqi attack.[10] This sequence of events moved US consciousness about the potential merits of BMD to the forefront.

When the United States once again offered Canada an opportunity to participate in BMD, a 1994 White Paper opened the door to an official government role. Senior officials in his department even told Defence Minister David Collenette that the new policy announcement would serve the purpose of a positive signal regarding BMD. Washington picked up the message and ran with it; NORAD renewal included a clause that enabled Canada to become involved in missile defence (Fergusson 2010, 156).[11]

When negotiations finally brought the Arctic Council into being at Ottawa in September 1996, the new entity reflected the US vision (Nord 2006, 306–7). It had a narrow, non-security mandate and would function as Washington had envisioned: as a forum for discussion and little else. Why, after much debate, did such a one-sided result, at great distance from Canadian preferences, occur? This is an appropriate point at which to reference once again the effects of a long-term trend, namely, Canadian near-abandonment of traditional military capability.

Canada, by the late 1990s, lacked the capacity to take significant military action—that is, it had very limited "hard" power and virtually none in comparison to the US (Hart 2008, 22–23; Hillier 2010, 331). Hard power refers to material capability: most notably, the capacity to deploy military force on land, by sea, and in the air. US observers in that era even compared Canada's military contribution to that of Iceland (Bothwell 2006, 513). Thus, from Washington's point of view, a disturbing question had come to the forefront: Could the Canadians be trusted to secure the Arctic? Given this doubt, it is not surprising that the US rejected Canada's vision of the Arctic Council as a multilateral forum for security cooperation. A lack of Canadian investment in Arctic security effectively encouraged American unilateralism.

Some observers in Canada also chided the government about a move toward soft power and away from hard power. A former Canadian ambassador to the US saw Ottawa as lacking in material resources to match up with its ideals regarding human security (Gotlieb 2004, 27). Chapter 2 covered the near moribund state of the CF in some detail; even more than rhetoric about human security, the lack of commitment of resources to the military—for whatever purpose—caused increasing doubts in the US during the 1990s about its northern neighbour's ability to provide basic security. Since the US tended not to rely even on its closest allies on security matters, the doubts probably justified a disposition that already existed against creation of an entity such as the Arctic Council.

Canadians had good reason to worry about US border–related concerns, in particular as the millennium drew to a close. The case of Ahmed Ressam created heightened sensitivity in Washington's corridors of power. Ressam took a ferry from Victoria, British Columbia, which docked in Port Angeles, Washington, on 14 December 1999. He travelled as Benni Noris and had "little difficulty obtaining false Canadian passports" (Thompson and Randall 2008, 306). US officials arrested him and found a car packed with explosives; Ressam had planned to blow up Los Angeles International Airport as midnight struck on 31 December 1999. Furthermore, he had been to Afghanistan for training in the "theory and practice of *jihad*" (Bothwell 2006, 502). Canada, as a result, now represented an increasingly prominent source of insecurity for the US.[12] US and Canadian officials discussed a security perimeter in light of the Ressam incident in December 1999, but this went nowhere beyond the talking stage (Barry 2007, 121).

For Can/Am security issues prior to 9/11, the context now is set. Five issues—border management, the Arctic, BMD, Iraq, and Libya—have been reviewed. It is time to assess the context of Can/Am relations, expressed through developments in the preceding matters, from the standpoint of four outlooks on security policy: realism, liberalism, the world of ideas, and the state and domestic politics.

Realism accounts effectively for security policy prior to the twentieth century. Can/Am relations in that era, with the border as the only active security issue, reflected great power rivalry and the quest for relative gains. The US, a rising power, challenged and ultimately surpassed Great Britain, Canada's patron, for supremacy on the North American continent.

From the twentieth century onward, the story shifts significantly to liberalism. The US and Canada built a security partnership following the rapprochement between London and Washington a century ago. Institutions intended to promote mutual security, border-related and otherwise, accumulated for Canada and the US over the course of the twentieth century. The most prominent among them are the International Joint Commission, CANUS Joint Board on Defence, NATO, and NORAD. Ottawa and Washington continue to pursue mutual gains to this day, with institutions widening and deepening, just as liberalism would anticipate.

Realism still echoes in the Arctic. While both countries generally pursue mutual gains in the domain of security, the Arctic is the exception for the US and Canada. Ottawa's long-standing efforts to assert sovereignty in the north create discomfort for Washington because of the indivisibility of the issue. Canadian reactions to a US presence in the Arctic sometimes become intense and even hostile. Ottawa's response to the voyages of the *Manhattan* and *Polar Sea* are prominent examples of Canadian nationalism coming to the forefront in defence of sovereignty.

From a realist point of view, the Arctic story in Can/Am relations makes good sense. The US perceives weakness and even (at times) irresponsibility on the part of Canada regarding Arctic security. Testing the waters, literally and figuratively, is what the US then does. Canada balances against the attempt of the US to exercise power in the Arctic through various means; legislation and devotion of greater resources are two of the observed techniques.

Ideas also matter, in conjunction with the government and domestic politics, in accounting for twists and turns of the Arctic issue. Sovereignty is an omnibus issue in Canadian politics. Concerns about a US takeover, in whatever form, never are far from the surface in the politics of policy making. Thus any Canadian government can be expected to take a strong stand, for reasons of political survival, if there is widespread public perception of US disrespect for Canadian sovereignty. Note that even Conservative governments, generally associated with a more pro-American point of view, do not remain silent when something such as the *Polar Sea* voyage—an event from Mulroney's time in office—comes along. In fact, Conservatives, with greater inherent vulnerability about the question of being too soft on the US, can experience even more pressure to be assertive regarding a sovereignty issue such as that of the Arctic.

BMD is an issue that brings together elements of realism and liberalism, along with the government and domestic politics interacting with the world of ideas. From the standpoint of realism, nothing is better than obtaining security from a trusted ally at no expense. In essence, that is the proposed BMD "deal" in terms of material commitment from Canada: a free good. This would enable Canada, if it accepted missile defence, to enjoy whatever security that would add while devoting resources to alternative purposes. In this context, given long-standing security cooperation, liberalism also would expect the answer from Ottawa to be "yes" regarding missile defence. BMD would just add another element to an existing collection of cooperative arrangements with the US. So, with relative and absolute gains available to be made, and thus realism and liberalism pointing in the same direction, why did Canada keep on saying "maybe" instead of "yes" to the US on BMD?

Domestic politics, intertwined with the idea of anti-Americanism as a major presence in Canadian culture, provides the answer. At various intervals, the government of the day found itself in a position to do one of three things. It could refuse BMD outright, which would annoy Washington. However, accepting BMD could mobilize xenophobic nationalism in Canada because the agreement involved a new weapon system that, at least in the eyes of some, did not have a strictly defensive purpose. BMD therefore, politically speaking, could be seen as a "bridge too far" in terms of integrating Canada with the US in continental security. Add the opposing forces together—factors reflecting (1) realism and liberalism on one side and (2) the government and domestic politics, along with the world of ideas, on the other—and the result is understandable: an intermittent Canadian response of "maybe" with regard to participation in BMD.

Limited Canadian involvement with Iraq and Libya, filtered through the US, is explained through a combination of realism and liberalism. On the liberal side of the ledger, Canada approved of the bombing campaign against Libya in 1986 because, as a US ally, Ottawa felt an obligation to stand together with Washington against terrorism. Canada also joined the multilateral military effort to evict Iraq from Kuwait in 1991. In both of these instances, elements of liberalism—cooperating with an ally against a state that flouted international law and joining in with a multilateral military deployment, respectively—are front and centre.

With regard to the realist side of the ledger, things point in the same direction. US action against Libya reflected an effort to use superior force to deter further aggression from a perceived rogue state that had supported terrorism. In the case of the Gulf War, the US and its allies believed they had no choice but to throw Saddam Hussein out of Kuwait. Failure to do so would leave him with a massively increased oil supply and create danger for Saudi Arabia and possibly other states in the region as well. Canada therefore endorsed Operation Desert Storm, which quickly and decisively evicted Iraq from Kuwait—but it did not participate in the first war against Iraq.

Causes

Events on 9/11 shook the world. When the airborne attacks occurred, Canadians reacted immediately and with great sympathy for Americans. The *Toronto Star* received more than 2,600 letters from readers offering condolences to the United States and, in Ottawa, "hundreds of Canadians attached small tributes to the iron railings around the U.S. Embassy: flowers, flags, notes, candles, and a birch bark scroll with 'God Bless America'" (Thompson and Randall 2008, 305). Anti-Americanism reached a low ebb, which created a window of opportunity for Ottawa. In responding to 9/11, the government would have much more flexibility than usual—especially a centre-left, Liberal government with a significant nationalist constituency that normally harboured suspicions about the US.

This section is less tidy than the one on causes from Chapter 2 because, in that instance, interest focused on effects in just one place: Afghanistan, with 9/11 as the cause and Canada going to war as the principal effect. The events of 9/11 triggered the Afghan war, which concluded in December 2001 with the eviction of the Taliban from power in Kabul. This shift in government ushered in a new stage of internal strife in Afghanistan, with a coalition of states led by the US fighting against a loose collection of adversaries to obtain stability. The war's conclusion also produced after-effects in security relations as a whole for the US and Canada. The changes observed have gone well beyond enhanced Canadian participation in the Afghan war.

For this chapter, the sense of 9/11 as a cause is more nuanced. The discussion that follows is brief because for certain Can/Am issues 9/11 did not serve as a catalyst for any particular effect. Instead, some of the assessment focuses on 9/11 as an enabling cause for significantly later events. Perhaps the metaphor of a toppling domino can be helpful here. The events of 9/11 represented a huge domino, toppling over many others after it. Some of those in the sequence are quite distant from yet still connected to the initial domino's fall. This, in essence, is how 9/11 had an impact on some of the events discussed later in this chapter and the next.

With regard to security, the border became Canada's immediate and principal concern after 9/11. Keeping the border open, given dramatically heightened US security concerns, represented a major challenge (Sokolsky and Lagassé 2006, 17). About 300,000 people cross the border every day. Various estimates put the value of trade at or over $1 million per minute. Thus the immediate US reaction to 9/11, from a Canadian point of view, created a waking nightmare (Lennox 2009, 115; see also Barry 2007, 116):

> Washington decided to put its border inspectors on a level 1 alert. In an instant, this action created a line of trucks thirty-six kilometres long at the Windsor-Detroit border crossing (to cite the most extreme example of many). Typically, making the crossing in one or two minutes, these trucks waited ten to fifteen hours. With $1.3 billion worth of goods crossing the border daily in two-way trade, the economic repercussions of such a security crackdown could not be taken lightly by either state in the continental system.

Even the brief border closure after 9/11 cost huge amounts of money. Some Canadian companies temporarily closed their operations (Barry 2007, 122). Even worse, rumours that the 9/11 hijackers had entered through Canada persisted in the US (Bow 2009, 132; Hart 2008, 226). Fortunately, key officials in Washington, if not the public as a whole, came to realize that accusations toward Canada regarding the terrorists had no basis in fact.

Events from 9/11 put Canada into a central location on the US "defense perimeter" (Clarkson 2002, 401); the terrorist attacks "highlighted the need for enhanced cooperation between nations to protect their citizens and their economies" (Baker 2006, 921; Lennox 2009, 119). Ottawa reacted quickly; Prime Minister Chrétien created an Ad

Hoc Cabinet Committee on Public Security and Anti-Terrorism, headed by John Manley (Barry 2007, 122). Bill C-36, a Canadian answer to the US Patriot Act, became law on 18 December 2001 (Lennox 2009, 12). The budget, moreover, included $7.7 billion over the next five years to improve border infrastructure and enforcement, along with $1.2 billion to strengthen the military.

Canada and the US signed the Smart Border Accord on 12 December 2001. The agreement covered a range of border-related issues, of which secure infrastructure, along with coordination and information sharing in enforcement of goals, is the most germane to our topic. Secure infrastructure provisions included improvements (key border points and trade corridors); intelligent transportation systems (featuring interoperable technologies); protection of critical infrastructure; and aviation security (comparability/equivalence of security and training standards) (DFAIT 2003).

With regard to coordination and information sharing, the Accord included provisions on integrated border and marine enforcement teams (e.g., expanding Integrated Border Enforcement Teams);[13] joint enforcement coordination; integrated intelligence; counterterrorism legislation and freezing of terrorist assets; joint training and exercises; and a range of technical matters (e.g., removal of deportees and sharing of data on fingerprints) (DFAIT 2003).

Canada also formed Integrated National Security Enforcement Teams in response to 9/11. The teams involved members from the RCMP and other security-related entities and began to form in major Canadian cities soon after the terrorist attacks. The judicial system added a prominent action of its own, to complement security-oriented measures described already; January 2002 featured a unanimous Supreme Court of Canada decision that an Iranian assassin could be deported on grounds of national security.

NORAD increased air patrols after 9/11 (Fergusson 2005a). Aside from such across-the-board measures, 9/11 had no immediate effect on the playing out of Arctic security as a Can/Am issue. In the short term after the attack, cooperation between Canada and the US in the GWOT overawed any tendencies toward conflict about a more circumscribed issue such as Arctic sovereignty.

BMD is the same type of issue as the Arctic at this stage; there are no immediate developments to report in response to 9/11. In fact, critics of BMD pointed toward the irrelevance of such a system in light of attacks from inside the US itself (Fergusson 2010, 215). At the same time, the events of 9/11 planted the seeds of later controversy over proposed missile defence. From the horror of that day emerged a heightened US sense of vulnerability (Fergusson 2010, 215). Washington became inclined to pursue security measures across the board and BMD re-entered the mix fairly quickly. The US naturally would look north of the border for support in this initiative when BMD came back onto the agenda. As one observer put it, after 9/11 "the writing was on the wall" with respect to the eventual need for a Canadian decision about BMD (Fergusson 2010, 217).

What, then, can be said about the remaining issues: the war in Iraq and the quite recent intervention in Libya as related to 9/11? The al Qaeda attack on 9/11 did not serve as a trigger for either of these interventions. Instead, the terrorist assaults of that day enabled these later events. As per earlier discussion, 9/11 looks like a huge domino that set in motion many others following after it. Consider, in that sense, the following process: in response to 9/11, Canada entered the Afghan war but had to pause its involvement because of a lack of both troops and war material. Ottawa then greatly increased its military capabilities and resumed a combat role at a much higher level through the deployment to Kandahar. Thus the CF had military resources available—at levels far beyond anything seen in decades—to make possible and even indirectly encourage a role in an intervention such as Libya. Moreover, the events of 9/11 and the resulting entry into the Afghan war changed Canadian culture as well. Opinion moved from a sense of national identity connected overwhelmingly with peacekeeping to a renewed openness to the application of conventional military force under well-defined and justified circumstances. For such reasons, later potential for Canadian involvement in Iraq and direct participation in Libya can be traced back (at least indirectly) through a series of steps to 9/11.

With this review of causes in place, attention turns to accounting for events. Once again, realism, liberalism, the world of ideas, and the government and domestic politics will be called on to account for what is observed.

Border security, the overarching issue of the day in the aftermath of 9/11, is multi-faceted. Elements of all the outlooks on foreign policy are present in how border security played out. Obviously, Ottawa had to act to protect the national interest, given the enormous economic losses that would have followed from any sustained closing of the border. The Canadian government followed the dictates of the national interest in the pragmatic manner a realist would have anticipated, resulting in the Smart Border Accord and other measures. Liberalism enters into the equation as well; Can/Am cooperation increased, with new legislation and institutions in the security domain. Bill C-36 and the security measures taken right after 9/11 in cooperation with the US figure prominently in that liberal part of the story.

Ideas, along with the government and domestic politics, combine
to complete the picture regarding border security. Canada's response to
9/11, in the specific context of continental security, can be seen in terms
of protecting sovereignty (Lennox 2009, 120). While Canada joined
forces with the US against terrorism, it also did so with caution and
attention to the desire—less pronounced in the US—to balance security
needs against potential problems arising with respect to civil rights. Thus
Canada attempted to preserve its sovereignty by taking measures necessary to ensure the US of its commitment to security but staying away, to
the extent possible, from any homogenizing effects arising from the fear
and anxiety in place after 9/11. This balancing act, of course, dovetails
with concerns based on domestic politics. While Ottawa had to cooperate with Washington, it also needed to draw limits to prevent a wave of
anti-government sentiment that could follow from what appeared to be
excessive conformity to US demands.

Can/Am relations in the Arctic were not directly affected by 9/11.
However, 9/11 did create the *potential* for a more realist-oriented policy
for Ottawa on that issue because of enhanced military capabilities. The
Canada that existed before 9/11 never could have considered the military measures in the Arctic that are described in the next chapter. The
9/11 attack also had an indirect impact on the decision about BMD that
later took place. Canada's involvement in Afghanistan created leverage
in the asymmetric relationship with the US, namely, the deployment
increased the feasibility of delaying in other areas and even ultimately
saying "no" to high-profile demands, especially when put forward in
a manner perceived as confrontational. BMD, as described in the next
chapter, serves as a prominent example of how that happened.

As with its influence on BMD and the Arctic, 9/11's impact on later
Canadian actions involving Iraq and Libya is indirect. Realism and the
world of ideas tell the short story here. As Canada built military capability rapidly after 9/11 and then participated in the Afghan war, it had
both the resources and the experience to re-engage in a more traditional,
realist pursuit of national security. Thus Canada gained the potential to
act in a more realist-oriented manner in the future—that is, to move
further away from human security and back to national security. With
regard to the world of ideas, preparations for war and experience in it
changed the Canadian mindset about security policy, at least in an incremental way. Human security diminished as a point of emphasis and was
replaced—implicitly, at first—with a more conventional pursuit of the
national interest. Moreover, this new direction could and did involve
military force if and when properly justified.

The Story So Far

Canada and the United States had significant contact, over several centuries, prior to their periods of independence. In an overall sense, the story of the relationship is accounted for by realism and then liberalism, respectively. Conflict over the border persisted for centuries and evolved into a more cooperative relationship throughout the twentieth century and beyond. The same can be said of Can/Am interactions over the much more specific matters of Libya in 1986 and Iraq in 1991. On both occasions, realism and liberalism pointed in the same direction. Canada supported its principal ally and acted in tandem with other states in the effort to evict Saddam Hussein from Kuwait. The context regarding BMD is mixed; there are elements of cooperation and conflict, with no real outcome forthcoming. This is not surprising when evenly matched opposing forces exerted by (1) realism and liberalism on one side and (2) the world of ideas intertwined with the government and domestic politics on the other are taken into account. Among the Can/Am issues concerned, only the Arctic features the persistent conflict anticipated by realism. This reflects the indivisible nature of sovereignty and thus the pursuit of relative gains by Ottawa and Washington. Domestic politics in Canada also reinforced Arctic tensions through public opposition to perceived US meddling.

The 9/11 attack stands as an immediate trigger of some significant developments and a more indirect cause for others. Canada cooperated right away with the US to meet its own principal security need—keeping the border open—and did so for reasons that reflected both realist and liberal thinking. Limits and nuances regarding Canadian integration with the US on border security are explained by the world of ideas in combination with the government and domestic politics. For the other issues—the Arctic, BMD, Iraq, and Libya—9/11 stands as a more distant cause that produced the potential for realist-oriented courses of action. In sum, 9/11 is most easily understood as a huge domino, with others toppling over after it—a story that continues in the next chapter.

Chapter 6

The United States:
Ally or Adversary?

How and Why?

Chapter 5 provided a historical context for security policy in the new millennium and also gave an account of 9/11 as a cause for change in security issues beyond the Afghan war itself. This chapter considers some key areas of interest: border management, the Arctic, BMD, the Iraq War of 2003, and Libyan intervention in 2011. Among these items, 9/11 either had a direct impact in a given area or set the stage for later developments, as per the domino metaphor from the last chapter.[1]

Characteristics

With the Taliban defeated and Afghan reconstruction underway, Can/Am security relations had reached a very positive place by early 2002. Prime Minister Chrétien met with President Bush in the Oval Office on March 14.[2] Bush thanked Chrétien for "steadfast support" in the GWOT and observed that Canadian troops had performed "brilliantly" in Afghanistan. The president described the border relationship as "great"—a model for the world. Bush viewed Canada as a "friend" and, quite pragmatically, as a supplier of energy; he characterized negotiations over softwood lumber (a much more high-profile issue in Canada than in the US) as moving along positively. Chrétien replied to the president in favourable-sounding generalities. Neither he nor Bush said a word about the building tension over possible US military action against Iraq (Chrétien 2008, 306). This public meeting may be viewed as the final public display of calm before the storm that picked up through 2002 and onward into the Iraq War of 2003.

Bush and Chrétien met again in Detroit in September 2002 (Goldenberg 2006, 286). By this time Iraq had "pushed Afghanistan off the public agenda" (Stein and Lang 2007, 52). Chrétien (2008, 310) reflected on the difficulty of his situation as the year drew to a close:

> the Americans kept preparing for war, in the face of strong resistance from France, Germany, Russia, China—and now Canada. All that autumn I was under increasing pressure to back the United States all the way—from Washington, from the business community, from the right-wing press, even from those Liberals who were in favour of military action or who opposed everything I did because they were supporting Martin's leadership bid.

Canada late in 2002 also featured intense *opposition* to involvement in military action aimed at Iraq. Demonstrations against participation in the US-led war plans against Iraq built up toward the end of 2002. About 2,000 people protested at Queen's Park in Toronto on November 16. Antiwar rallies occurred in Ottawa and other major cities soon after.

Antiwar momentum in Canada made the situation for Chrétien increasingly difficult. His closest ally wanted Canadian support, but the proposed intervention lacked a UN mandate. This shortcoming created a fundamentally different situation than Afghanistan a year earlier; privately, the prime minister agreed more with the protesters than the president in reacting to the potential Iraq venture. In his memoirs, Chrétien (2008, 308) recalls urging the British prime minister, Tony Blair, to exert influence on Bush to put the brakes on a war that lacked a supporting UN resolution. The Canadian prime minister and other prominent members of government stayed "on message" throughout the buildup to war: Canada remained committed to the UN and multilateralism across the board.

Regardless of rising tensions over Iraq, Can/Am security cooperation proceeded apace in other areas. Northern Command (NORTHCOM), located within NORAD at Peterson Air Force Base in Colorado Springs, became operational on 1 October 2002 (Thompson and Randall 2008, 308; Fergusson 2010, 218). This new authority had as its purpose the integration of security for the continental US. NORTHCOM, in a word, created institutional momentum on the Canadian side of the border as well.

Canada and the US produced a new agreement about security cooperation on 9 December 2002. The document reaffirmed the importance of NORAD and followed naturally from the advent of NORTHCOM. The two governments established a Bi-national Planning Group (BPG) at NORAD headquarters in Colorado Springs. This BPG would have the following mandate regarding military planning, surveillance, and support to civilian authorities:

• preparing contingency plans to respond to threats and attacks, and other major emergencies in Canada or the United States;
• acting to prevent and mitigate threats or attacks through:
  ○ maintaining awareness of emerging situations through maritime surveillance activities;
  ○ sharing maritime intelligence and operational information in accordance with national laws, policies, and directives; and
  ○ assessing maritime threats, incidents, and emergencies in order to advise and/or warn governments;
• designing and participating in exercises;
• conducting joint training programs;
• validating plans prior to approval; and
• establishing appropriate coordination mechanisms with relevant federal agencies.

Source: Graham 2008

Most striking about this list is its breadth and depth. While the BPG did not represent a military force in and of itself, its examination of scenarios would have a significant impact on operations shared by Canada and the United States. In addition, the BPG extended security cooperation significantly into the maritime domain.

BMD, as apparent already, comes in and out of the story regarding Can/Am security relations. Its role can be downright confusing. In his memoirs, former prime minister Paul Martin (2008, 385) described the positions of the former Canadian prime ministers, collectively speaking, as representing "studied ambiguity." Against the backdrop of the BPG, US efforts to promote Canadian participation in BMD resumed and created a new stage of studied ambiguity and building tensions. Perhaps most confusing of all is the fact that Washington's desire for mere approval from Ottawa, as opposed to more material demands, had sufficient symbolic importance to cause great difficulty for the Canadians in responding decisively on BMD.

Ongoing uncertainty about BMD becomes obvious in light of the meeting on that subject, requested by *Canada*, in January 2003. A Canadian delegation met with the US Missile Defence Agency in search of information about a possible BMD system. For reasons of security, the

Missile Defence Agency could not offer much in return, so the meeting did not produce any substantive outcome. However, by taking the initiative here, Ottawa fed the impression in Washington that it would be interested in, and possibly agreeable to, BMD (Fergusson 2005a).

Tensions mounted in the Can/Am security relationship as Washington's pressure on Baghdad increased into 2003. Protests against Canadian involvement in an attack against Iraq escalated in February 2003. Substantial demonstrations took place in many communities across the country. Especially notable, given the weather conditions—with wind chill, -30 degrees Celsius—is the protest in Montreal. More than 100,000 people came out to oppose the war in spite of the extreme cold. On March 15, two days before Chrétien's announcement of his decision about Canadian participation, a quarter of a million people demonstrated in Montreal against an Iraq War. Substantial demonstrations continued to take place in other Canadian cities and poll results consistently came out against participation in the upcoming US-orchestrated attack. Aside from the rallies leading up to the referenda about Quebec sovereignty in 1980 and 1995, the frequency and intensity of these events dwarfed any other expressions of public sentiment via demonstrations in recent memory.

Bush's campaign against Iraq continued to lack both the legitimacy of the UN and support from NATO. Instead, Washington had put together something known as the Coalition of the Willing that included Great Britain as a principal ally and many lesser countries with largely symbolic rather than military value. Privately, Chrétien harboured great skepticism regarding the US rationale for invasion, notably as related to the presence of WMDs in Iraq. Consider his recollections about the evidence from US intelligence and the high-profile speech by Secretary of State Colin Powell at the UN in February 2003:

> I wouldn't have been able to convince a judge of the municipal court in Shawinigan with the evidence I was given. Indeed, when Colin Powell presented his government's case to the United Nations the following February, I knew he was on very thin ice indeed. From what I had read, I figured he had been sold a bill of goods.

Under these conditions, Canada tried to "play the role of an honest broker" and "work out a diplomatic solution" that could prevent war (Chrétien 2008, 312, 313).

Ottawa's situation became increasingly difficult as the deadline for war drew near. Canada, in the words of the prime minister's chief of staff, existed as "closely intertwined with the United States" and thus "faced a difficult decision" under pressure from its neighbour (Goldenberg 2006, 6, 288). Ottawa needed to show solidarity with Washington after 9/11, but Canadian leaders wondered whether the Iraq invasion would "bring about more democracy in the Middle East, or whether it would be responsible for provoking more terrorism in the world" (Goldenberg 2006, 288). Canada "waffled in public" over Iraq (Jockel and Sokolsky 2008, 104). Government statements reflected this ambivalence: highly negative about the war in public but more encouraging with Washington in private (Stein and Lang 2007, 90). In the end, the Canadian decision against membership in the Coalition of the Willing came as a surprise to the US because of these mixed signals (Bow 2009, 140).

While Canada did not join the US war effort in Iraq, this hardly represented the most important aspect of its decision making on the issue. Canadian support had been more important to the US symbolically than substantively (Thompson and Randall 2008, 310). One observer points out that collateral damage ensued as a result of the *way* the decision had been made as opposed to its content: "our politicians often looked like deer caught in the headlights, as each new development presented another opportunity to publicly disagree with the United States. Safety tip: when disappointing a friend, try not to make things worse" (Welsh 2004, 41). The errors of commission are summarized below (Bow 2009, 145–46):

> Canada didn't just say no to war in Iraq; it also publicly questioned the White House's case for intervention, actively campaigned for a compromise solution within the Security Council even in the face of clear US opposition, chose not to warn the US before announcing that it would not support the war, and then delivered the decision in the form of a public rebuke.

These actions made little or no sense when directed toward "one's closest friend and ally" because the affronts, collectively speaking, looked like what would be meant for an adversary (Fergusson 2010, 232).

Interesting to ponder, given the intensity of Ottawa's response to Washington, is the domestic setting of the decision against going to war. The war clearly would have been especially unpopular in Quebec (Doran 2006, 400–1; Jockel and Sokolsky 2008, 105). Some observers even see the persistent references by the prime minister to the importance of UN approval as a matter of political convenience in the time leading up to the Iraq War (Hart 2008, 29).

Another dimension of the Iraq decision concerns participation in Afghanistan. Canadians generally opposed the Iraq War. Thus the Afghan mission, "in terms of Canada's liberal internationalist brand and . . . trad-itions as . . . peacekeeper, seemed an appropriate role for the Canadian military" (Sjolander 2009, 85; see also Jockel and Sokolsky 2008, 104). Heading up ISAF in Afghanistan could pay off in multiple ways; it repre-sented "a real opportunity for Canada to show international leadership" and "would help get Canada off the hook on Iraq" (Stein and Lang 2007, 71). In particular, the prime minister could plead a lack of military resour-ces as a credible excuse for staying out of the Iraq War (Bow 2009, 145).

Different reactions to the decision against fighting in Iraq came from the Canadian military. General Henault and Vice Admiral Maddison had preferred Canada in Iraq rather than Afghanistan because of an expecta-tion that the US would win in about six weeks (Stein and Lang 2007, 61). This reaction is consistent with a sense of US realization that the Canadian military would not have been needed in Iraq. The CF's limited capacity and increased costs of coordination if it had become involved suggest that Canadian military contributions did not factor into US cal-culations about Iraq. Instead, the US hoped for diplomatic approval from Canada, along with other states, because it lacked the institutional support that had been present for Afghanistan (Bow 2009, 134).

Canada ultimately *did* participate in the Iraq War, albeit in limited, unofficial, and possibly unintended ways. Exchange officers with the US and Great Britain stayed in place at the CF's request; this occurred in spite of attacks from the media and in the House of Commons (Stein and Lang 2007, 89; Lennox 2009, 102). In February 2003, Canada took command of TF 151, which operated from the Persian Gulf through the Strait of Hormuz. Controversy ensued. Chrétien, in response to crit-ics, asserted that TF 151's mandate concerned only the Afghan war and anti-terror–related activities (Stein and Lang 2007, 81, 85). It is inter-esting to note that, as a non-participant in official terms, the five ships from Canada exceeded its contribution of three to the Gulf War of 1991 (Lennox 2009, 108).

After Saddam Hussein had been deposed, Canada offered $300 mil-lion to the US for Iraqi reconstruction (Lennox 2009, 108). Under pres-sure from Washington, Ottawa "sent the RCMP to help train Iraqi police and Elections Canada to help run the voting there. It also participated in the NATO Training Mission in Iraq" (Jockel and Sokolsky 2008, 106; see also Bow 2009, 159; Lennox 2009, 109). Moreover, the Canadian naval role in the Arabian Sea stood as "one of the largest from a NATO member" (Sokolsky and Lagassé 2006, 17). These forms of involvement may have reflected a shift in public opinion about Iraq after the conven-tional phase of fighting concluded in a quick victory for the Coalition of the Willing. After the decision in March, the Canadian public backed off somewhat from its antiwar stance. A survey in April 2003, for example, revealed that a majority of respondents viewed diplomatic support for the US as something that would have been appropriate (Bow 2009, 142).

Whether in the domain of security or otherwise, no evidence exists of US retaliation aimed in response to Canada's decision against full-fledged participation in the Iraq War (Bow 2009, 129). Consider, for example, Canadian vulnerability regarding the border. On 16 April 2003 the US announced that Canadians would be *exempt* from laws requiring people coming in and out of the country to register with customs officials (Welsh 2004, 45; see also Bow 2009, 128, 155). Chrétien (2008, 315) spoke with Andrew Card, chief of staff to the president, and received assurances that Bush had been disappointed rather than angry with Canada. Moreover, while the prime minister acknowledged in his memoirs that Bush's scheduled visit to Ottawa in May had been cancelled, he cites that as happening by "mutual agreement" (Chrétien 2008, 315). Given the timing, it made sense for the two leaders to keep a low profile with each other; specifically, the prime minister recalls his concern about massive antiwar protests and general awkwardness in the aftermath of the Canadian decision against Iraq (Chrétien 2008, 315–16).

Chrétien also felt pressure to support BMD to maintain the ongoing bargain with the US on security. Together with this desire to improve relations with Washington, however, existed public pressure to avoid any agreement identified with a president so unpopular among Canadians (Fergusson 2010, 232). So the prime minister tried to be noncommittal on BMD (Thompson and Randall 2008, 304). Chrétien played for time when he rose in the House of Commons to speak about missile defence, not wanting to increase tension any further. He referred to a "debate" on BMD and gave no specifics (Lennox 2009, 84). On 29 May 2003, the minister of DND, John McCallum, announced in the House of Commons that Canada would enter into discussions with the US on BMD, although with the qualification that "weaponization" of outer space would be unacceptable (quoted in Fergusson 2005a).

Discussions took place in the fall of 2003 as the Chrétien government came toward the end of its days. According to the prime minister, the debate had "less to do with [BMD's] logic than with its practicality and consequences" (Chrétien 2008, 302). Canada would be in the middle of things vis-à-vis any missile attack simply by virtue of its location. Concerns existed about expense and whether a missile shield would work. To some degree a BMD system seemed overtaken by events as well: What good would it do in an era when terrorists could and did attack from inside national borders?[3] With so many points of uncertainty, Chrétien passed the decision about BMD along to Martin, his successor.

Consider the January 2004 letter from Minister of DND David Pratt to US Secretary of State Donald Rumsfeld vis-à-vis mixed signals on BMD. The Canadian government initiated this contact to inform the US that it wanted to have the early warning function of missile defence assigned to NORAD. Rumsfeld publicly agreed; at that point, according to one well-informed observer on the matter of BMD, "everyone believed that Canada had essentially said yes" (Fergusson 2010, 207). Studied ambiguity, indeed!

Martin visited Washington on 29 April 2004. At the Woodrow Wilson Center he mapped out his views on Canada and the world. The prime minister obviously hoped to improve relations with the US, which had become shaky in the aftermath of the Iraq War decision. However, with regard to BMD participation as a potential positive gesture toward Washington, Martin faced an increasingly hostile climate at home. An internal Liberal Party poll from February had revealed 70 percent in favour of BMD, but that dropped throughout the year and reached 56 percent *opposed* in a poll from November 2004 (Fergusson 2010, 246). Caution naturally ensued regarding any dramatic pro-American gesture in light of the deepening dislike, even hatred, for George W. Bush among key sectors of the Liberal constituency. Given its minority position from the June 2004 election onward, the Martin government had to tread very carefully on issues that could be used to mobilize opposition (Fergusson 2010, 246). BMD, in that context, would be perfect for NDP efforts to pull away Liberal support on the left.

Revealing are priorities at National Defence Headquarters when Bill Graham took over at DND in July 2004, which focused on NORAD and BMD, along with getting more money (Stein and Lang 2007, 132). An August 2004 agreement allowed NORAD to "transmit tactical warning and assessment of ballistic missile launches to missile defence command and control" (Sokolsky and Lagassé 2006, 18; see also Kite and Nord 2007, 263; Fergusson 2005a, 2005b; Lennox 2009, 85). All of these developments served as generally positive signals regarding the future prospects for Canada's participation in BMD.

Recollections from the prime minister confirm that concerns about NORAD played a key role in security policy at the time (Martin 2008, 386):

Preserving NORAD was my priority, and I wasted no time after the spring 2004 election in making the necessary changes to the NORAD agreement through an exchange of letters with President Bush. The result of the new arrangement was that NORAD would share access to tracking data on incoming missiles, which the Americans might use on their own for managing the BMD system.

In light of these observations, it becomes easy to see how US expectations regarding participation by Canada in BMD would build up in what appeared to be highly visible, if incremental, steps toward saying "yes."

Advocates of BMD in the new round noted its defensive nature and the fact that the US had offered it for free (Canada 2006b, 79–80). Ottawa continued to hedge on a decision regarding BMD through the spring of 2004 (Lennox 2009, 85). Worries about how the US might view Canada as an ally had mounted in public debate in late 2004 and early 2005. NORAD, as suggested already, might be endangered if Canada stayed out of BMD (Stein and Lang 2007, 122–23).[4]

Both sides had agreed not to raise the issue of BMD during Bush's visit to Canada in December 2004 (Lennox 2009, 86). Bush, however, criticized Canada in a speech given at Halifax on 1 December 2004. He chided Canadian waffling on BMD and refusal on Iraq. When Bush took the issue of BMD to the public in this way, his action created an "embarrassing situation" (Thompson and Randall 2008, 317). The president had angered Martin by going back on the deal to stay quiet about BMD for the time being (Stein and Lang 2007, 166; Martin 2008, 388; Fergusson 2010, 248). Bush effectively "provoked Martin with an impromptu call for Canada to join the United States" (Bow 2009, 159).[5] Moreover, the demand came against the backdrop of an especially high level of anti-Americanism among Canadians as a by-product of the Iraq War and its violent aftermath.

Critics mobilized right away and Martin faced problems in his divided Liberal caucus (Hart 2008, 94; Lennox 2009, 87). Martin had favoured BMD but ended up saying "no" in spite of many signals in favour. For example, just two days before the announcement against BMD, Canada's ambassador to the United States, Frank McKenna, observed that Canada had been participating already—a position Ottawa quickly repudiated (Fergusson 2005a).

Martin shocked and angered the US, in turn, by rejecting BMD (Kite and Nord 2007, 263; Fergusson 2010, 207). On 24 February 2005, Foreign Minister Pierre Pettigrew announced in the House of Commons that Canada "would not participate" (Fergusson 2005a). This decision had aspects that even the government, eager to distance itself from the unpopular Bush administration, did not fully comprehend. Ottawa effectively had said "no" to future negotiations, as well, when it refused an important draft memorandum of understanding. Rejection of the memo prevented "Canadian access to missile defence research development and testing" that "would have had great value for Canadian strategic interests" (Fergusson 2010, 207).

Refusal to join in on BMD "sent a loud signal to the White House that Canada was not prepared to follow through on difficult issues and begin to build an agenda looking to the future of the relationship" (Hart 2008, 95; see also Fergusson 2005b, 65, and Fergusson 2005a). Ottawa's decision "injected a severe chill into what had been expected to be a more cordial, if not more productive, dialogue" (Burney 2005, 12). The US "felt insulted that it was being used as a crass tool to gain votes in Canada" (Fergusson 2010, 254). Washington naturally had higher expectations regarding the centre-right Martin as a replacement for the centre-left Chrétien. This made the disappointment all the greater. However, anti-Americanism had reached a high point in Canada as a result of the Iraq War in particular and perceptions of George W. Bush in general. Potentially harmful distortions in security policy followed from the need for Canadian leadership to take into account that profile of opinion.

From the prime minister's point of view, the situation regarding BMD looked quite different—perhaps bordering on impossible to manage. Martin (2008, 387) describes the period leading up to Canadian refusal as one of great difficulty. The prime minister claims that either DND or US Department of Defence officials had been "stalling" on his requests for information about BMD. He also explicitly references the "increasingly shrill" opposition across Canada to BMD (Martin 2008, 387, 388). In looking back on the decision, Martin points out a conundrum regarding the trip Bush made to Canada in December 2004 and its politically harmful by-products: "In retrospect, it might have been wiser to declare my intentions on BMD in advance of his visit, but that also ran the risk of embarrassing the president" (Martin 2008, 388). The ferocity of Martin's refusal comes into context when he observes that the public pressure from Bush in his December speech "infuriated me" (Martin 2008, 388).

From the standpoint of Washington, BMD represented Ottawa at its worst—in the words of one *Canadian* observer, "only the latest example of its inclination to seek a free ride" (Hart 2008, 168). However, the US did not retaliate against Canada. Instead, Ottawa's refusal caught Washington by surprise because it would have been so easy, given the zero financial burden involved, for Canada to assent. Canada, in fact, had been seen as irrelevant to missile defence in operational terms (Stein and Lang 2007, 175–77). Mere agreement to BMD had been the only thing Washington really wanted, given that Canada existed, regardless, under the continental defence umbrella. Thus Washington might be described as baffled rather than furious as a result of Martin's choice of "telling the Americans off" over accepting a free gift in the domain of security.

Critics have harsh words for the decisions against Iraq and missile defence. These actions introduced "uncertainty" to relations with the US (Macdonald 2005, 59) and even "loss of access and influence in Washington and a further step down the road to irrelevance" (Hart 2008, 139–40). These decisions certainly affected Canadian thinking about Afghanistan when Washington approached Ottawa later on in 2005 about coming back in at a higher level of intensity. The choice of Kandahar, with its attendant high demands and dangers in comparison to prior Canadian involvement, is connected to saying "no" to the US on Iraq and BMD.

Concerns about possible US reactions to Canadian refusal of BMD, however, had become "exaggerated" in the eyes of some observers (Sjolander 2009, 86n13). The prime minister confirms this point in his memoirs: "while it was clear to me that President Bush would like us in, I never had the impression that it was crucial to our overall relationship—nor did my officials at the PMO and PCO" (Martin 2008, 389). Nevertheless, Ottawa announced $12.8 billion for the CF over five years to cushion the shock of saying "no" to BMD (Lennox 2009, 87).

The Martin government's International Policy Statement (IPS) from 19 April 2005 provides a window into Ottawa's thinking about security-related matters beyond Afghanistan. Reactions to it varied. Some viewed the IPS as not amounting to much at all; one observer summed it up as coupling "stirring rhetoric and timid action" (Hart 2008, 96; see also Kite and Nord 2007, 265, on continuity within IPS). The document called explicitly for Canada to take on a role of pride and influence in the world (Travers and Owen 2008, 687). Some regarded the IPS as a signal of important change, most notably an impending emphasis on security and defence (Fitzsimmons 2009, 4). If so, this could signal a new phase of convergence in policy, with Canada "increasingly linked" to the US in continental security (Kite and Nord 2007, 273).

Observers at the time also noted the prominent role in the IPS of the CF, which had been marginalized previously. The IPS hinted at a role for the CF that would go far beyond traditional peacekeeping. With regard to the US and security coordination, while the IPS did not mention a security perimeter explicitly, that concept seemed "present beneath the surface" (Fergusson 2005b, 63).

Most notable as a point of agreement about the IPS among observers is its explicit acknowledgement of the existence of, and need to act upon, national interests (Bercuson and Stairs 2005, 3; Bercuson 2005, 4). Pragmatic references to interests in the IPS replaced the previously featured status for projection of Canadian values abroad, which had reached its crest in the Axworthy years. For example, the IPS heavily emphasized the Arctic and concerns about sovereignty (Carnaghan and Goody 2006, 7).

Critics, however, attacked what appeared to be a residual presence of unmatched means and ends in the IPS. Nossal (2005, 42) urged a "responsibility to be honest" in reaction to the IPS's articulation of very expansive goals that remained in line with the doctrine of "responsibility to protect" as put forward in tandem with the UN. Another critic noted the absence of a "procurement plan" (Hobson 2005, 95). Could Canada expect to take bold action with no apparent plan for obtaining the means to do so?

Events moved forward in line with the general position, conveyed by the IPS, in favour of a more prominent Canadian role in international security. Canada Day in 2005 witnessed the creation of Canada Command (CANCOM). This entity provided an "integrated structure to optimize the employment of Canadian Forces (CF) at home or abroad through a single commander" (Macdonald 2005, 55). Even apparently domestic security actions such as this one, however, ended up impinging on relations with the US; CANCOM, as noted at the time of its creation, would "need to liaise closely with US forces whenever a crisis is cross-border in nature" (Granatstein 2005, 74; see also Macdonald 2005, 58). In particular, that meant coordination with NORTHCOM (Fergusson 2005a). As CANCOM moved forward, care would be needed "to ensure that the NORAD baby is not thrown out with the bathwater as a new bilateral defence relationship becomes better defined" (Macdonald 2005, 59). In spite of conflicts over Iraq and BMD, the advent of CANCOM revealed that Can/Am security integration at an institutional level had obtained greater breadth and depth than ever.

From the Conservative Party of Canada came a federal election platform for 2006 titled *Stand Up for Canada*. The title of the document foreshadows its contents in the realm of security and thus the position of what soon would become the Harper government. While the Liberal government under Martin had reversed the downward trend in military spending and appointed the activist General Hillier as CDS, the Tory platform advocated further movement toward restoring a more traditional role for the CF and the means to carry it out. In a section titled "Defending Canada," for example, the platform claims that "successive Liberal governments have undermined and underfunded Canada's Armed Forces" (Conservative Party of Canada 2006, 45).

The Conservative Party of Canada refers to the transformation of the CF in *Stand Up for Canada*, its plan for defending Canada. The emphasis is on increased funding. Arctic sovereignty and security are mentioned as well. The basic point that comes across is that Canada would be better

Conservative Party of Canada: The Plan for Defending Canada

A Conservative government will:

- complete the transformation of military operations and defence administration;
- recruit 13,000 additional regular forces and 10,000 additional reserve forces personnel;
- increase spending on the Canadian Forces by $5.3 billion over the next five years, beyond the currently projected levels of defence spending;
- expand recruiting and training, reduce rank structure overhead, review civilian and military HQ functions, and increase front-line personnel;
- increase investment in base infrastructure and housing for our forces;
- acquire equipment needed to support a multi-role, combat-capable maritime, land, and air force. Fundamental capability requirements are national surveillance and control, counter-terrorism, air and sea deployability, and logistics supportability;
- increase the Canadian Forces' capacity to protect Canada's Arctic sovereignty and security;
- restore the regular army presence in British Columbia; and
- treat Canada's veterans with the respect and honour that they deserve, and ensure better responsiveness to veterans with a Veterans' Bill of Rights and a Veterans' Ombudsman.

Source: Conservative Party of Canada 2006, 45

served with a focus on national as opposed to human security. Enhanced military capability therefore becomes a priority.

Stephen Harper became prime minister on 23 January 2006 and remains in office at this time, with a majority government since 2 May 2011. His ascent to office, even with just a minority government at the outset, meant that the new emphasis on security and defence would receive, if anything, a further boost. Harper's words from the beginning of his time as prime minister reflected the Tory election platform on security policy summarized above. A typical speech by Harper, delivered in Kandahar on 13 March 2006, emphasized Canadian "defence and security policy" (Hart 2008, 71). Harper's ongoing statements in favour of an enhanced CF paralleled Canada's rapidly increasing military involvement in Afghanistan. All of this reflected the reality of greater integration of purpose and action with the US in a military-based struggle against the forces of terrorism. At the same time, Canadian public opinion regarding a security perimeter with the US remained divided, with exactly 50 percent in favour according to a poll from 2005 (Potter 2008, 160).

The issue of BMD continues to be delicately handled in the Harper era of government. Harper did specify conditions for Canadian participation just prior to taking office: a North Korean ability to attack North America with a nuclear weapon (Massie 2013). However, as an ideological conservative with vulnerability to charges about being too close to the US, Harper dropped the issue of BMD quickly. In short, he had other, more important security-related fish to fry, specifically, the Arctic.

Released by the Library of Parliament three days after Harper's election, a document titled *Canadian Arctic Sovereignty* sent a direct message about Ottawa's intentions regarding the Far North. Sovereignty would be front and centre (Carnaghan and Goody 2006, 1) because of

> potential incursions into Canadian Arctic territory . . . airspace, surface (terrestrial and maritime), and sub-surface (by nuclear submarines). Canada's ability to detect and monitor such territorial incursions and to enforce sovereign claims over its Arctic territory in such cases has been questioned. . . . [M]any observers believe . . . the Northwest Passage, the shipping route through Canada's Arctic waters, will be open to increased shipping activity in the coming decades as the ice melts. . . . It is important to note that the Arctic is a vast and remote territory that presents many difficulties in terms of surveillance, regulation, and infrastructure development.

The document obviously takes a firm position on protection of sovereignty. It justifies attention to the Arctic across the board as a result of climate change in particular—an interesting usage of an issue normally associated with the political left to argue for policy change in a direction usually advocated by the political right.

Taken from *Canadian Arctic Sovereignty*, "Canadian Strategic Capabilities in the Arctic" enumerates Canada's surveillance and air, land, and sea capabilities. The document's listing of capabilities, interestingly enough, appears right after the word *incursions* is used to describe the presence of "French, British, Russian, and especially American nuclear submarines" (Carnaghan and Goody 2006, 8). The word *especially* in relation to the US is revealing; Russia, the only non-ally in the group, is not singled out in this way. The mindset regarding the Arctic focuses on the capability to deter and even confront intruders.

Shifting emphasis toward military-based protection of Arctic sovereignty in an official document such as this one is revealing because of its timing. A comprehensive statement such as *Canadian Arctic Sovereignty*, which appeared right at the beginning of Harper's time in office, obviously must have been prepared during the Martin government. The emphasis on military capability and protecting sovereignty, put forward in language that sounds like traditional pursuit of national interests, reinforces the

Canadian Strategic Capabilities in the Arctic

- The Canadian Coast Guard operates a fleet of five icebreakers that guide foreign vessels through Canada's Arctic waters and assist in harbour breakouts, routing, and northern resupply. . . . The Canadian Navy does not currently have the capacity to operate within the Arctic ice.
- The Canadian Forces Northern Area (CFNA) is headquartered in Yellowknife. CFNA headquarters comprises 65 Regular Force, Reserve, and civilian personnel. CFNA military activities per year include two "Sovereignty Operations (Army)," two "Northern Patrols" (flights of Aurora patrol aircraft), 10–30 "Sovereignty Patrols" (CFNA), and one "Enhanced Sovereignty Patrol." As part of the Canadian Forces Transformation, CFNA will assume a greater command and control function. CFNA will become the "Northern" regional headquarters of the new Canada Command in 2006.
- Within the CFNA, the Canadian Ranger Patrol Group provides a military presence in northern and remote areas by conducting patrols, monitoring Canada's northern territory, and collecting information. These part-time reservists comprise a significant element of Canada's northern presence.
- As part of the North American Aerospace Defense Command (NORAD), Canada maintains a chain of unmanned radar sites, the North Warning System, which provides limited aerospace surveillance of Canadian and United States Arctic territory. In addition, Canada's Department of National Defence recently announced the creation of Project Polar Epsilon, which "will provide all-weather, day/night [surface] observation of Canada's Arctic region," using information from Canada's RADARSAT 2 satellite, by May 2009.

Source: Carnaghan and Goody 2006, 8–9. Reproduced with the permission of the Library of Parliament, 2012.

point made earlier about Harper building on a trend already in place under Martin. Canada would move further away from human security and toward national security, with the Arctic as a featured issue.

Harper wasted no time in putting forward an assertive position regarding the Arctic. On 25 January 2006, remarks by US Ambassador David Wilkins either forced or provided a welcome opportunity for Harper to speak out. The ambassador came out against Harper's proposal to put military icebreakers in the Arctic. Harper told reporters the next day, "the United States defends its sovereignty and the Canadian government will defend its sovereignty. It is the Canadian people we get our mandate from, not the ambassador of the United States" (CBC 2006). Harper even told the ambassador to refrain from commenting further on Arctic sovereignty (Nord 2007, 207). These assertions had heightened intensity as a result of coming from a politician ordinarily identified with relatively pro-American thinking.

Events on the other side of the globe also reinforced the new reality of Canadian security policy. For many years, the US had taken the lead in military action, with Canada identified as the peacekeeper on the North American team. A further sign of change in those purely defined roles took place in Israel with a changing of the guard in a UN operation. CF participation in Operation Danaca in the Golan Heights ended on 24 March 2006. So came to an end Canadian participation in UN peacekeeping, at least for the time being. This operation, part of a UN peacekeeping mission on the Golan Heights since 1974, had been terminated by direction of the previous Martin government. The new Harper regime presided over Canadian withdrawal (Shadwick 2006, 94).

Meanwhile, movement toward integration in continental security received a boost. When the BPG's mandate expired on 12 May 2006, it issued a final report. The BPG asserted that "an overarching vision for continental defence and security organizations was missing" (Baker 2006, 92). Identified through analysis from Baker (2006, 92–93), a summary of the most important recommendations from the BPG is provided. Together, these recommendations give a sense that, in spite of all the tensions involving Canadian refusal regarding Iraq and BMD, the perceived need for greater security integration with the US remained intact. The BPG, for example, recommended more routinized sharing of information, along with setting a mutual agenda regarding essential tasks in security.

Summary of Recommendations from BPG

- The provision of a deliberate planning agreement articulating specific responsibilities, the goals needing to be accomplished, and how often Canada-US plans should be updated;
- the development of a nation-to-nation information sharing agreement, shifting defence and security partners from a "need-to-know" to a "need-to-share" paradigm. Supporting plans, processes and procedures would be developed in support of this information-sharing agreement;
- the development of a communications-needs definition, which will help eliminate operational gaps, shortfalls, and duplications amongst NORAD, Canada Command, and US Northern Command across the air, maritime, and land domains; and
- the development of a common interagency, intergovernmental, and bi-national Combined and Joint Mission Essential Task List to support a joint and combined multi-year exercise program that could synergize efforts in defence and civil support.

Source: Baker 2006, 92–93

Further to the general point regarding integration of security are other more specific manifestations of that trend. Renewal of NORAD in May 2006 included "new responsibility for maritime warning" (Kite and Nord 2007, 263). In addition, a Canadian government report from 2006 called for Integrated Border Enforcement Teams to be expanded from 23 to at least 30 (Canada 2006b, 40). Concerns about keeping the border secure and assuaging Washington's concerns obviously remained at the forefront.

Events focused on counterterrorism are revealing with respect to evolving Canadian attitudes that, in turn, affected the feasible and even likely set of outcomes for Can/Am security issues as the decade moved forward. Prominent in the Canadian experience are the events of 2 June 2006. Efforts by police and security services revealed a terrorist scheme of major dimensions that culminated on that day in a series of raids in Metropolitan Toronto. These actions produced 18 arrests and subsequent convictions in 2010. The Toronto 18, as they became known, had elaborate plans that included truck bombs; attacks on the Canadian Broadcasting Corporation, Parliament, and Canadian Security and Intelligence Service headquarters; taking hostages; and even beheading the prime minister and other political leaders.

Interesting to ponder, in light of this success on the part of the Canadian security apparatus, is public reaction. Canadian perception of threat *increased* to 71 percent following prevention of all attacks planned by the Toronto 18 (Harvey 2007, 295). Two polls soon after produced virtually identical numbers: 57 to 58 percent of respondents regarded those apprehended as the "tip of the iceberg" (Harvey 2007, 297). Why, then, would such negative reactions ensue? "The Canadian media," as Harvey (2007, 296) observes, "fed public fears by explaining the threat with reference to, among other things, the inevitable backlash against Canada's commitment to Afghanistan, serious gaps in Canada's immigration and refugee policies, fundamental flaws with Canadian multiculturalism, and so forth." The public imagination clearly had switched away from human security, with greater openness to new priorities based on national security in light of experience with violent threats.

What, then, becomes the net result of an ongoing atmosphere of concern about terrorist attacks, even well out of proportion to their probability of happening? Demands for increased safety are not satiated by greater spending but instead persist even in the face of successful efforts by the government to prevent terrorism (Harvey 2007). This mindset is compatible with greater government activity in an overall sense, which includes a willingness to spend much more money on the CF and other security-related resources than in the past.

Security coordination with the US, as a by-product of Canadian demand for safety, expanded throughout the years after 9/11 with very little protest aside from the ultra-high-profile issues of Iraq and BMD. Consider, for example, the Tri-Command Vision as a realized tangent from the unrealized BMD. This entity integrates the "complementary visions" of NORAD, NORTHCOM, and CANCOM.

Table 6-1 summarizes the Tri-Command's missions. In reviewing each mission, note the obvious interdependence that exists and presumably builds with time as actions accumulate. For example, NORAD hardly would be able to conduct aerospace control for North America without cooperation from CANCOM, given that the latter entity is responsible for detecting threats to Canada (NORAD, NORTHCOM, and CANCOM 2006). Other points of comparison for any pair of these organizations would produce the same conclusion; they all are part of the same alphabet soup of Can/Am security, in practice, as opposed to acronyms representing entities that can or do operate separately. A sense of highly integrated security comes across in the stated goals, as well, which include strengthening collective ability to deal with threats, improving unity of effort, developing a culture of "continuous collaboration and cooperation," enhancing "intelligence and information sharing," and working together to assist civil authorities (NORAD, NORTHCOM, and CANCOM 2006). The degree of integration observed arguably renders prior Canadian refusal to join BMD in an official capacity all but irrelevant.

According to one expert observer, since July 2006, the three commands have been "working closely to study and improve their understanding of each other's roles, missions, and responsibilities with the aim of eliminating gaps and redundancies, while strengthening daily military

Table 6-1   Tri-Command Missions

Group	Mission
NORAD	Conducts persistent aerospace and maritime warning and aerospace control to defend North America.
NORTHCOM	Anticipates and conducts Homeland Defense and Civil Support operations within the assigned area of responsibility to defend, protect, and secure the United States and its interests.
CANCOM	Conducts operations to detect, deter, prevent, preempt, and defeat threats and aggression aimed at Canada within the area of responsibility. When requested, Canada COM will provide military assistance to civil authorities including consequence management, in order to protect and defend Canada.

Source: DFAIT 2011a

cooperation in the defense of North America" (Renuart 2009, 95). Note in particular the word *redundancies*. This is especially interesting in the context of integration via perimeter security. Put differently, elimination of redundancies implies a reduced level of independence for each actor. While efficiency is promoted in this way, a by-product is further *inter*-dependence in Can/Am security.

Obvious in this narrative on Can/Am security relations, by now, is an overall trend toward integration in spite of specific disagreements. Arctic sovereignty, in that sense, continued as an irritant in spite of the electoral shift in Canada to a presumably more pro-American Tory government. Canada's single most important question regarding Arctic sovereignty and security remained ocean navigation (Parker and Madjd-Sadjadi 2010, 337). (This continues as a priority in spite of the possibility that Arctic transit shipping could be 60 to 75 years away [Canada 2006a, 88].) Canada claims the route for the possible Northwest Passage because it is less than 20 kilometres distant from Canadian islands. Washington's counterclaims regarding international waters continue to vex Ottawa. The Arctic sovereignty conflict thereby creates very odd combinations of actors: for one, the US and Canada on opposite sides. For another, Canada also quarrels with Denmark, another NATO ally, over Hans Island. Meanwhile, the US and EU oppose claims by Canada and other states, notably Russia, based on the sector principle.

Canada began to back up rhetoric about the Arctic with military deployment soon after Harper came to power. On 12 August 2006, the CF launched Operation Lancaster. This 12-day exercise in the Eastern Arctic demonstrated a commitment to sovereignty (Canada 2006a). "The North," the prime minister observed, "is poised to take a much bigger role in Canada's economic and social development." Harper added, "We must ensure the unique ecosystem of the North, and the unique cultural traditions of the First Peoples of the North, are respected and protected" (Canada 2006a). Note the hybrid nature of these comments; from a political standpoint, those on the right would be pleased by the assertion of national interest through a long-absent military presence, while the left would approve of the message tacked on about protecting the environment and Aboriginal cultures.

Harper followed up with additional resources for the CF in the Arctic. At Resolute Bay on 10 August 2007, the prime minister announced the following measures:

- expansion of the size and capability of the Canadian Rangers up to 5,000 personnel, with upgraded and modernized vehicles, weapons, and uniforms;

- creation of a CF Arctic training centre; and
- an establishment at Nanisivik, a facility for deepwater docking and refueling.

The prime minister stated explicitly that he intended these measures to "significantly strengthen Canada's sovereignty in the Arctic" (Canada 2007). If and when realized, the level of Canadian commitment to the Arctic as described by Harper would be unprecedented.

One unfolding aspect of the Arctic is revealed in a high-profile report from the US Geological Survey in 2008; it projected "undiscovered oil reserves in the Arctic circle to be 90 billion barrels and 44 billion barrels of natural gas liquids" (Broadhead 2010, 925). In addition, based on three mines in the Arctic, Canada recently became the third largest producer of diamonds in the world (Canada 2010, 9). These and other developments with economic implications for the future continued to stimulate the Arctic as a point of contention in Can/Am security relations.

Launched on 14 December 2007, Canada's Radarsat-2 satellite followed Radarsat-1. This new satellite, delayed several years because of controversies with the US, finally took orbit and stood as a major accomplishment of the Canadian Space Agency. The US had expressed concerns that enemy states might be able to purchase images of the US, so the project moved, it might be said, out of the US orbit. Radarsat-2 therefore represented another step forward in the Canadian take-charge attitude regarding the Arctic. By increasing its surveillance capabilities in the Far North through the Canadian Space Agency, Canada counteracted US claims that it could not be trusted to secure the Arctic.

Along those lines, Canada continued to conduct Arctic military exercises. The CF started Operation Nunalivut in the spring of 2008. This operation entailed air surveillance and Canadian Ranger patrols. It took place on the west coast of Ellesmere Island, between Canadian Forces Stations Alert and Eureka (Parker and Madjd-Sadjadi 2010, 344). Such areas previously had not witnessed a significant ground presence from the CF.

CF activity in the Arctic reflected the new government's priority for national over human security. Consider the trend line revealed by the *Canada First* Defence Strategy released on 12 May 2008 (DND 2008). The prime minister's message on the first page of this document emphasizes the government's commitment to the CF through acquisition of "urgently needed equipment such as C-17 Globemaster transport aircraft" (DND 2008, 1). The executive summary of *Canada First* goes on to say that the statement "provides the planning certainty required to allow the Government to continue rebuilding the Canadian Forces into the state-of-the-art military that Canada needs and deserves" (DND 2008, 3). With regard to the strategic environment, Canadians are said to "live in a world characterized by volatility and unpredictability." On that same page, along with the challenges posed by terrorism, is a paragraph on Arctic sovereignty and security (DND 2008, 6). Ensuing pages emphasize national security and being a "reliable partner" with the US in defence of the continent (DND 2008, 8). The document also includes a justification for expenditures on the CF in terms of likely benefits from technology and innovation, with potentially valuable commercial applications (DND 2008, 20).

The CF has six core missions in Canada, in North America, and around the globe. The agenda is vast and emphasizes national security; the closest it comes to mentioning human security is the offer of support to civilian authorities faced with the need for disaster relief. The Arctic and NORAD are mentioned in the very first of the six points regarding ongoing needs for domestic and continental security (DND 2008, 3). Short- and long-term deployment of the CF outside of Canada is identified as a core mission as well.

Plans for investing in the military over a long period, conveyed in detail by *Canada First*, include "personnel, equipment, readiness and infrastructure" (2008, 2). A series of major proposed investments from *Canada First* dwarf prior defence commitments at any time since World War II. Most notable, perhaps, is that the procurements clearly go beyond capabilities required for the peacekeeping activities that had been the conventional place of the CF in previous decades. *Canada First* also refers to the ability to sustain military operations—an implicit

Canada First Defence Strategy: Six Core Missions

- Conduct daily domestic and continental operations, including in the Arctic and through NORAD;
- support a major international event in Canada, such as the 2010 Olympics;
- respond to a major terrorist attack;
- support civilian authorities during a crisis in Canada such as a natural disaster;
- lead and/or conduct a major international operation for an extended period; and
- deploy forces in response to crises elsewhere in the world for shorter periods.

Source: DND 2008, 3

Canada First: Investments in the Canadian Forces

- Increase the number of military personnel to 70,000 Regular Forces and 30,000 Reserve Forces;
- replace the Forces' core equipment fleets, including: 15 ships to replace existing destroyers and frigates; 10 to 12 maritime patrol aircraft; 17 fixed-wing search and rescue aircraft; 65 next-generation fighter aircraft; and a fleet of land combat vehicles and systems;
- strengthen the overall state of the Forces' readiness to deploy and their ability to sustain operations once deployed; and
- improve and modernize defence infrastructure.

Source: DND 2008, 4

reaction, at least, to the lack of staying power revealed by the initial deployment to Afghanistan.

Policy statements from Harper continued to emphasize Arctic sovereignty. Perhaps the strongest statement to date occurred in Tuktoyaktuk on 27 August 2008: "if you are in Canada's Arctic you will be playing by Canada's rules" (Harper quoted in Canada 2008). Harper justified this vigilant reaction in terms of "record numbers of ships" in Canadian Arctic waters as a result of the retreating ice pack. The prime minister announced the intention to "expand the reach" of the Arctic Waters Pollution Prevention Act; if successful in this venture, Canada would double its jurisdiction to 200 nautical miles. Specifically, the government also announced that it would amend the Canada Shipping Act to "require all vessels entering Canadian Arctic waters to report to the Canadian Coast Guard's NORDREG [Northern Canada Vessel Traffic Services] reporting system" (Canada 2009a). This represented a movement far beyond the voluntary reporting in place at the time.

Given the unilateral bent of the US under George W. Bush's administration, the US reaction to ongoing Canadian efforts toward exercising Arctic sovereignty is not without humour, albeit unintentional. The US Embassy expressed the desire to ensure that "any enhanced protection of the Canadian Arctic marine environment is achieved in a manner that is consistent with the international law of the sea" (quoted in Canwest 2008). The US Embassy spokesperson went on to emphasize, more positively, a forthcoming joint seabed mapping expedition in the Arctic (Canwest 2008; "US, Canada to Map Unexplored Arctic Seafloor" 2008).

President Bush issued a Presidential Directive on US interests in the Arctic on 13 January 2009. "The United States," Bush asserted, "is an Arctic nation, with varied and compelling interests in the region" (redOrbit 2009). His further remarks emphasized security: "Preserving the rights and duties relating to navigation and overflight in the Arctic region supports our ability to exercise these rights throughout the world, including through strategic straits (redOrbit 2009). Thus Bush reasserted US claims, contrary to the long-standing Canadian position, regarding the right to traverse the Northwest Passage.

DND announced on 4 July 2009 that Radarsat-2 would be used more for security purposes that included coastlines and the Arctic. Soon after, the prime minister made another security-related visit to the Far North. On 19 August 2009, Harper came to observe the military component of Operation Nanook 09, described as "a major whole-of-government exercise designed to build Canada's capacity to assert Canadian sovereignty and respond to emergencies throughout the Arctic" (Canada 2009c). Minister of Defence Peter MacKay and CDS General Walt Natynczyk joined Harper on the trip. From August 6 to 28, the CF maintained a visible land, sea, and air presence in the vicinity of Baffin Island. Harper described the operation as "a valuable training opportunity for Canadian Forces personnel" and proof of the "capacity and resolve necessary to assert our Arctic sovereignty over land, sea and air" (Canada 2009c). The very next day the prime minister announced construction, in Pangnirtung, Nunavut, of a new small craft harbour. A news release described Pangnirtung as a "key outpost on Canada's Arctic shoreline" (Canada 2009b).

Canadian efforts to assert Arctic sovereignty continued apace in 2010. June of that year brought an explicit call from a Parliamentary Standing Committee (Canada 2010, 17) to "expedite" procurement of Arctic ships for DND, with emphasis on building the promised *John G. Diefenbaker* icebreaker to permit delivery within 15 years. When visiting Allen Bay, near the far northern community of Resolute Bay, Harper announced on 25 August 2010 that Canada would deploy a new, third generation of Radarsat satellites. The cost would be $487 million and the satellites are to go into orbit by 2015 (Ibbitson 2010).

Unlike Chapters 3 and 4, which found a natural break point between characteristics and consequences with the end of an Afghan combat role for Canada in July 2011, the current chapter's multi-issue agenda does not lend itself to such an obvious date. Some of the issues, such as the Iraq War and Libyan intervention, are over in the sense of immediate Canadian involvement. This facilitates assessment of consequences. However, other issues are ongoing. Although Canada said "no" to BMD in the last decade, that does not mean the US never will ask about it again. The border is a never-ending issue and, of course, Arctic sovereignty is in the midst of a period in which change is coming quickly.

For such reasons, the break point for characteristics and consequences regarding Can/Am security relations is set arbitrarily at the end of 2010. While many other dates could be suggested, this choice makes sense for an assessment completed about one year later. In other words, events from 2011 are deemed contemporary and thus a good approximate set of data points to use in assessing consequences.

With that break point in place, it is time to assess the characteristics of Can/Am security policy. As per the usual practice, the four outlooks of realism, liberalism, the world of ideas, and the government and domestic politics will be used to account for the characteristics observed for border management, the Arctic, Iraq, and BMD. Canada's experiences with Libya, which do not start to heat up until the consequence stage, will also be discussed in this section.

Border management reflects a straightforward combination of liberalism with realism. In a realist vein, Ottawa's policy showed pragmatism. It cooperated with the militarily superior US to keep the border open to the greatest degree possible. Initiatives such as NORTHCOM and Tri-Command can be seen in this context; through such arrangements, Canada counteracted possible US concerns about its northern neighbour's commitment to continental security. Ottawa thereby made itself look like a much less risky bet, on the security front, than it had previously. Such arrangements, of course, also are consistent with a liberal emphasis on institutions. From that point of view, developments such as NORTHCOM and Tri-Command reflect the widening and deepening of an already trustworthy relationship involving Canada and the US.

Arctic sovereignty is an issue readily accounted for by a combination of realism and the world of ideas. Among Canadians, US presence in the Arctic elicits a nationalist, even hostile, response. Although for varying reasons, Canadians across the political spectrum can be counted on to support the idea of Arctic sovereignty. The Harper government, which wanted to emphasize national over human security in the domain of policy, utilized the Arctic as justification for enhancement and use of military capability. The Tories, for example, deployed satellite technology for improved surveillance and held military exercises on a regular basis in the Far North.

Canada's difficult decision to stay out of the Iraq War reflected a complex combination of factors pushing and pulling back and forth. From a realist point of view, the war would make sense in one way but not another. The US, as an overwhelmingly powerful ally, wanted Canada to join the war against Iraq. Yet the Canadian government and public, generally speaking, did not believe in the relatively limited evidence about a threat to security posed by WMDs. Thinking based on liberalism goes back and forth in the same way: on the one hand, Canada already had extensive security cooperation with the US and membership in the Coalition of the Willing would be just another instance. On the other hand, the keyword in the preceding sentence is *just*. For the majority of Canadians, an invasion of Iraq went against liberal values based on working out problems through institutions because the UN had not given that US-led venture its blessing.

Ultimately, a combination of ideas, along with government and domestic politics, proved overwhelming when the time came for a decision about Iraq. Ideas mattered and argued strongly against the war. Chrétien (2008, 319), for example, observed that the decision against Iraq showed that "Canadians had held firm to our values as a keeper of peace through multilateral institutions, no matter how great the threats and uncertainties we faced." Domestic politics also appeared to play a key part in the outcome.[6] The war had evoked in the public mind highly negative stereotypes about the US regarding aggressive action. An attack on Saddam Hussein, in spite of the appalling nature of his regime, did not make sense to the public in the context of available evidence about why this should be done from the standpoint of security. Add to that the very high level of dislike for George W. Bush in particular and Ottawa increasingly found itself with no viable choice, politically speaking, other than to stay out of war.

Canada's agonizing process of decision making and ultimate choice against BMD also reflected the operation of factors from all four outlooks. Realism and liberalism pointed toward participation. From a realist standpoint, saying "yes" to BMD cost nothing and gained favour with the world's most powerful state, which also happened to be located next door to Canada. In the eyes of liberalism, BMD would represent a further increment in an already established institutional network of Can/Am cooperation in security.

Factors pushing in the other direction, however, eventually ended up deciding the matter against participation in missile defence. Domestic politics factored significantly into the rejection of BMD according to most observers (Fergusson 2010, 251). BMD had become associated with the increasingly unpopular George W. Bush, so political safety argued against participation with the passing of time. Martin had to worry in particular about the youth wing of his party, which adamantly opposed the venture. He also had a potential problem with the NDP; eschewing BMD would protect against the NDP's ongoing efforts to pull away support from the left wing of the Liberal Party (Fergusson 2010, 251). The prime minister's anger at the president for pushing too hard on BMD in a public rebuke delivered in Canada itself settled the matter.

When referring to Canada's experiences with Libya, it once again makes sense to return to the domino metaphor. The weight of events throughout the decade continued to shift in a direction that made policies such as military intervention, which reflect at least to some degree a realist mindset, increasingly viable for the Canadian government. As will become apparent, the Canada that existed prior to the post-9/11 buildup of the CF could not have participated in the Libyan intervention in the militarily effective way that it ultimately did.

Consequences

Significant consequences followed from Can/Am security experiences of the last decade. Integration of policy increased notably from an already high base. Canadian military capabilities grew substantially and emphasis shifted to applying the CF to national rather than human security. Ongoing Canadian efforts to assert Arctic sovereignty, along with the role in Libya during 2011, may be seen as consequences of the developments just noted. Canada, as a by-product, also had to deal with new dimensions of security policy that reflected economic realities imposed by recession and domestic politics. Finally, the Canadian mindset regarding Can/Am relations and security policy in general have changed significantly as a result of experiences since 9/11. Each of the preceding consequences is reviewed in further detail.

One highly visible consequence of 9/11 is the qualitatively higher degree of integration in Can/Am security regarding the border and a host of other matters. Announced on 4 February 2011 by Harper and Obama, a new security and prosperity initiative contained sweeping priorities and recommendations.[7] The declaration, which came during the prime minister's visit to Washington, referred directly to a "perimeter approach to security." It also noted that the US and Canada expected "to use a risk management approach where compatible, interoperable, and—where possible—joint measures and technology should proportionately and effectively address the threats we share" (USA 2011). Key areas of cooperation listed by the declaration included addressing threats early (e.g., matching biometrics that permit immediate sharing of information on travellers); trade facilitation, economic growth, and jobs (e.g., integrated cargo security strategy); integrated cross-border law enforcement (e.g., cross-designated officers); and critical infrastructure and cybersecurity (e.g., implement a cross-border approach to strengthen resilience). These priorities culminated in the announcement of a Beyond the Border Working Group (USA 2011).

It is virtually beyond the pale that such integration would have been witnessed in the absence of the shattering events of 9/11 and its aftermath.

Another consequence of Canadian experience since 9/11 is greatly enhanced military capability. While examples are legion, CFB Wainwright is especially illuminating. The base is located in Denwood, Alberta. As the training location for the PPCLIs, CFB Wainwright includes the Canadian Manoeuvre Training Centre. The Centre is a state-of-the-art facility that reflects a major shift in favour of readiness for the CF as a fighting force. It uses a Weapons Effects Simulation System that includes advanced technology. All of this is a far cry from the world of the CF in the 1990s.

With regard to the Arctic, one consequence of the last decade of interaction is that the Northwest Passage is entrenched as the central security-related conflict with the US (Dyment 2010, 98). Revitalized CF capabilities have made it possible for the government to pursue a national security agenda, with emphasis on sovereignty, in the playing out of the Northwest Passage issue in particular and the Arctic in general (Broadhead 2010, 928). War games have been played in the Far North each summer over recent years. In addition, the Tory government's promise to back up Arctic sovereignty through various means is in place to a significant degree already: three armed icebreakers; a national sensor system; a promise of Arctic surveillance; a new Arctic training centre at Resolute Bay; additional Canadian rangers; an airborne battalion and lift capacity; up to eight polar class 5 Arctic offshore patrol ships; refurbishment of the deepwater port at the former mining site in Nanisivik on Baffin Island's Borden Peninsula (Broadhead 2010, 920).

With greatly increased military capabilities, wartime experience in Afghanistan, and enhanced Can/Am security coordination in place, Ottawa's role in the Libyan conflict of 2011 emerges as a natural long-term consequence of 9/11. Libya, in that sense, may be just the latest domino to fall over as a result of events set in motion a decade ago. Perhaps the most striking aspect of the Can/Am collaboration in what follows is the degree to which old-style US leadership, with Canada dragged along into anything that resembled military action, is entirely absent. In terms of overall resources deployed, France and Britain led the way, with the US not taking on most of the burden as it had in so many other deployments.

Gadhafi's regime had become increasingly embattled by the outset of 2011, and the CF played an essential role in helping Canadians and some others to escape Libya in February of that year. On 28 February 2011, two CC-130J Hercules and two CC-177 Globemaster strategic airlifters stood ready to begin the evacuation (Chaplin-Thomas 2011). Operation Mobile commenced soon after and removed 191 people from

Libya (DND/CF 2011). These actions demonstrated government willingness, along with the CF's new-found ability, to operate on the other
side of the world with significant and rapid airlift.

Not without good reason did such actions take place, as Gadhafi
ordered increasingly violent repression of popular protests against his
regime. The Canadian government supported both UN Security Council
(UNSC) Resolutions 1970 and 1973:

- UNSC 1970 aimed to halt Gadhafi's repression without threat or use
  of armed intervention; and
- UNSC 1973 authorized action to protect civilians, but not occupation of Libya.

Canada moved in tandem with the UN; on February 26, it instituted
(1) a freeze on assets in Canada held by the Libyan government and (2)
a ban on financial transactions with either the government of Libya or
associated agencies and institutions (DND/CF 2011).

Gadhafi defied UN measures to rein in his repressive actions. Canada
joined with the team effort, which featured NATO members, to deploy
military resources against Libya to protect those in dissent. Canada
deployed the HMCS *Charlottetown* and CF-18 Hornet aircraft during
March to the Mediterranean. The jets joined with those of other states
in pursuit of an operation named Odyssey Dawn to enforce UNSC
Resolution 1973 (DND/CF 2011).

Canadian involvement with the Libyan venture, in spite of its blessing
from the UN, evoked criticism from a public already feeling the burden
of ongoing military commitments to the Afghan war. Criticism from
the political left started right away and persisted throughout Canadian
involvement in Libya. Policy analysts writing from a more pragmatic
point of view looked at the growing Canadian role with a skeptical eye
(Burney 2011, 1):

> And why Canada? We are already doing much of the heavy-lifting
> in Afghanistan whereas several NATO allies have taken a pass. Is
> it because we were snubbed for a Security Council seat and want
> to re-establish our credentials for "peace-keeping"? Is it because
> we regard ourselves as an architect of the Responsibility to Protect
> concept adopted by the UN? If so, where will it lead—to Iran?
> Zimbabwe? North Korea? There is a long wait list.

Visible in this summary view is the building sense of dissatisfaction with
NATO, discussed at some length in Chapter 3, regarding fulfilment of

military responsibilities. Given previous Canadian free riding on the US in that domain, the quotation effectively reveals how much had changed in Canada by the time Libya came to the front of the international agenda. Just a decade earlier it would have been unlikely for Canada to be among the military leaders in an overseas operation and unthinkable that its political commentators would be taking other states to task for not using sufficient force.

Consider the extent of Canadian involvement as a "top player in the military intervention," with "15 aircraft, one warship, more than 500 military personnel, special forces and a NATO commander" (Meyer 2011). Lieutenant General Charles Bouchard from the CF had command of the expanding NATO operation against Gadhafi. Canada's participation included using air power against ground targets and taking an "aggressive posture" regarding rules of engagement (Meyer 2011). Moreover, at the NATO meeting on June 8 and 9, Minister of DND Peter MacKay announced that Canada had spent $26 million already on Operation Mobile (Canada 2011f).

Parliament agreed to extend the Canadian mission to Libya, with near-unanimous support, soon after the NATO meeting in June. Only Green Party leader Elizabeth May voted against the motion. The Tory government secured overwhelming support in the House of Commons by emphasizing two points: promises to (1) boost humanitarian aid and (2) recognize the rebels as legitimate representatives of Libya's citizens. Given fatigue with Afghanistan, the government had to assure the Liberals and NDP that ground troops would not be used in Libya to secure their support.

Canada continued to coordinate with other states in the attempt to support the Libyan opposition and weaken the Gadhafi regime's capacity to engage in repression. In July, DFAIT Minister John Baird met with the Contact Group on Libya in Istanbul, Turkey. Discussions focused on humanitarian assistance from Canada and other states. On August 8, Canada expelled all remaining Libyan diplomats from Ottawa and on August 27 Baird hinted at Canadian military involvement continuing beyond the September 27 mandate (DFAIT 2011d; Payton 2011).

Events at home served as a reminder that the new security policy, with its more activist approach toward deployment and use of force, would have to exist within resource-related limits. While Harper had promised even back in the election campaign of 2005 to provide new vessels to DND for Arctic deployment, he had to delay this once again quite recently on account of economic realities imposed by the world-wide recession. Delivery of the first "ice capable" vessel of a set of three vessels—$3.1 billion Arctic offshore patrol ships—now is expected in 2015. This delay almost certainly reflected limited capacity for the maritime procurement system of DND, which until recently had been little used.

Present also in the process of upgrading Arctic military capacity is competition, with a political tone, regarding contracts. The premiers of Nova Scotia (Darrell Dexter) and British Columbia (Christy Clark), along with transport critic Michel Guimond (Bloc Québécois), spoke up on behalf of contracts for shipyards in their respective provinces (http:// navaltoday.com, 6 July 2011). Thus other elements in the Canadian federal system, most notably provinces, would try to have their say in how the CF would be equipped and supplied in the new era of enhanced capability.

Libya continued to heat up politically into the fall season. With the rise of the National Transitional Council as a realistic possibility for an interim government, Canada announced on September 1 that it would lift all sanctions against Libya and unfreeze assets (Canada 2011d). In a statement on September 13, Baird announced that Canada, in light of the "situation on the ground in Tripoli," would re-establish its diplomatic presence in Libya by opening a temporary embassy (DFAIT 2011f). Soon after, on September 26, the House of Commons voted 189 to 98 to extend Canada's "United Nations-sanctioned, NATO-led military mission in Libya" (DFAIT 2011b). Canada ultimately had 655 troops, seven CF-18 fighter jets, three refueling aircraft, and the HCMS *Vancouver* as part of Operation Mobile, which officially came to a close on October 28. By that time, Canadian aircraft had carried out approximately 10 percent of NATO missions over Libya (defenceWeb 2011).

Canadian deployments played a significant role in the Libyan military operation right through to victory for the rebels on October 20. At that time the final Gadhafi stronghold of Sirte fell and the former dictator met a quick end at the hands of rebel forces. An editorial in the *Globe and Mail* regarded the outcome as a significant political victory for the prime minister: "Mr. Harper can now expect some vindication in public opinion for his arguments for a muscular Canada, with military assets and the will to deploy them" (Clark 2011). In the more conservative *National Post*, an editorial cited the victory in Libya as evidence of the need to keep investing in the CF. By past Canadian standards, criticism of the military role in Libya appeared relatively muted, at least from the standpoint of opposing the use of force as a matter of principle.

With regard to the nation-building front, the *Ottawa Citizen* reported that Canada would give $10 million to the new Libyan government for various security-related purposes. Baird announced on October 22 that Canada would focus on helping to rebuild and develop Libya's economy (CBC 2011). These commitments, while smaller in size, paralleled those made by Ottawa to the nascent Afghan state—a reflection of the understanding that victory in battle is not sufficient to put a stable democracy in place of a sordid old regime.[8]

Among the consequences of a decade that featured significant developments in Can/Am security relations, the least tangible may turn out to be the most important. Consider, in that sense, the following question about values: Did the events in Can/Am relations that ensued from 9/11 fundamentally change the Canadian mindset, which had focused on human security and peacekeeping, to one that primarily emphasized national security?

The "Statement by the Prime Minister of Canada on the End of the NATO-Led Libyan Mission" conveys the remarks given by the prime minister on October 28 at the close of Operation Mobile. The statement focuses on the brutality of the Gadhafi regime as grounds for its overthrow but does so without mentioning human security as a concept. The CF, along with NATO forces in general, are praised for their performance in the operation. Taken together, the components of the statement reflect a new vision of Canadian activity abroad. While quite willing to coordinate with Washington and other allies, note that Harper's statement does not single out the US. It would be difficult to find a more revealing, yet subtle, reflection of the change that had occurred in the Can/Am security relationship. Paradoxically, while in one way more *inter*dependent with the US than ever, Canada also acted in a more *in*dependent manner, as a purveyor of national security, than witnessed in recent decades.

Reflections on Canada and the United States

While significant events occurred in other decades of Can/Am security relations, it would not be an exaggeration to say that the last one had more memorable developments than any other 10 years in living memory. Border management, the Arctic, Iraq, BMD, and Libya combined to reinforce some existing traits of Can/Am security relations while bringing about dramatic change in others.

With regard to continuity, the two allies elaborated existing structures for cooperation and instituted new ones as well. By the time the decade concluded, the institutional basis of Can/Am security cooperation had expanded dramatically. At the same time, the Canadian contribution to the partnership altered significantly as a result of the experience in Afghanistan. A subsequent Canadian military buildup over the last

Statement by the Prime Minister of Canada on the End of the NATO-Led Libyan Mission

28 October 2011
Ottawa, Ontario

Prime Minister Stephen Harper today issued the following statement on the close of the NATO-led mission:

With the Libyan people having freed themselves from the Gaddafi regime, Canada's military mission in Libya is complete and Canadians can be proud of the job well done by our troops.

Since the onset of the crisis in Libya, Canada has played a critical role both politically and militarily to protect innocent civilians against a cruel and oppressive regime.

Working alongside our NATO allies, the Canadian Armed Forces established and maintained a no-fly zone under United Nations Security Council Resolution 1973. The Canadian Armed Forces were instrumental in mission success, flying over some 1500 military missions. Their performance is a tribute to their training and leadership and a result of having the right equipment to get the job done.

I also want to reiterate my congratulations to Lieutenant-General Charles Bouchard and commend him for his pivotal role in leading the combined NATO military mission. He has represented our country with distinction.

We saw a blatant wrong being perpetrated by a brutal regime and took a leadership role with our allies to help set it right. As a result, Colonel Gaddafi's 42 years of oppression have come to an end and Libyans now have an opportunity to create a more secure, just and peaceful country.

While our military mission in Libya has come to an end, Canada will continue helping Libyans by supporting their efforts to build a brighter and better future for themselves. Canada recently announced it would be contributing $10 million to help secure weapons of mass destruction and remove and dispose of explosive remnants of war.

Source: Canada 2011e

decade produced mixed results from a US perspective. Canada participated in the Afghan war and the Libyan intervention as a solid partner for Washington. However, Ottawa said "no" to both Iraq and BMD. In addition, during the Harper era, Canada twisted the eagle's beak in the Arctic. Perhaps the more militarily capable and experienced Canada that emerged from the last decade may be viewed as more assertive with its US neighbour even as it became increasingly interdependent in terms of security. Given long-standing American complaints about Canadian free riding on security, the preceding observation is not without irony.

Chapter 7

A "Model Citizen" on the World Stage

More than any other decade in history, the last 10 years have featured events with major consequences for Canadian security policy. For a nation that survived two world wars and other significant challenges over more than 13 previous decades, that is a big assertion. Nevertheless, this chapter asserts that the decade since 9/11 has *transformed* Canadian security policy.

This final chapter offers tentative answers to the questions that inspired this book. It begins with the most general query of whether Canadian security policy is different than it was before 9/11 and, if so, how? The answer, of course, is "yes," and in various ways that add up to a transformation (although as we will see, there are some aspects of continuity). I then consider whether Canadians have an accurate sense of their place in the world. Other topics include an assessment of Canadian decision making and how it might be improved in the future, the ways in which Canada may be unique, and Canada's likely future direction in security policy.

Is Canadian Security Policy Different than Before?

Without question, 9/11 transformed Canadian security policy. Previous chapters confirm a wide range of developments. Among the most important are

- an upgrading of the CF in both physical and psychological terms;
- greater security integration with the US;
- simmering tension with the US in the Arctic; and
- abrupt decline in NATO as Canada's principal alliance.

Consider first the CF in both material terms and its place in Canadian society. Table 7-1, taken from the *Canada First* policy statement of 2008, outlines a plan for defence expenditures for 2008–9 to 2027–28. By previous Canadian standards, the numbers are extraordinary: $490 billion overall. It almost goes without saying that political realities, most notably as related to available finances and the disposition of future governments, can throw even a well-planned initiative such as this one into disarray. Thus the Tory plan conveyed in Table 7-1 may never be

Table 7-1   *Canada First* Defence Strategy, Total Defence Spending, 2008–9 to 2027–28 (Accrual Numbers)

Pillar	Amount	%	Remarks
Personnel	$250B	51	70,000 Regular and 30,000 Reserve personnel by 2028; includes 25,000 civilian workforce
Equipment			
Previous Announcements	$15B[a]	3	Previously announced equipment purchases, including:
			• C-17 Globemasters • C-130J Hercules • Arctic/Offshore Patrol Ships • CH-47F Chinook Helicopters • Trucks
New Major Fleet Replacements	$20B[b]	4	• Fixed-Wing Search and Rescue Aircraft • Destroyers and Frigates • Maritime Patrol Aircraft • Fighter Aircraft • Land Combat Vehicles and Systems
Other Capital	$25B	5	Includes individual weapons, communications equipment, etc.
Infrastructure	$40B	8	Increased investment in rebuilding and maintenance of infrastructure of approximately $100M/year
Readiness	$140B	29	Approximately $140M/year in new spending on spare parts, maintenance and training
Total Spending over 20 Years	**$490B**	**100%**	

Source: Adapted from DND 2008, 12, chart 3

[a]This figure reflects only the capital component of this equipment over the 20-year period. The previously announced total of $30B includes the capital and in-service support costs over the full life of the equipment.

[b]This figure represents the capital costs of the new Major Fleet Replacements during the 20-year period reflected in the chart. The total capital costs of these platforms amortized over their useful life, which extend beyond this 20-year period, amount to $45–50B.

completed. At the same time, even if the precise numbers in the table do not come to fruition, the trend line in the allocation of resources is clear to see. The CF once again is a significant player in Ottawa.

Take, for example, what is planned for personnel. The $250 billion allocation for personnel that appears in Table 7-1, 51 percent of the total, is orders of magnitude beyond what would have appeared a decade earlier. At that time critics of Canadian security policy, with General Hillier emerging as most prominent among them, had observed that the CF lacked the capacity to act. A dearth of physical capabilities, starting with personnel, ruled certain policy options out of hand. The table, by contrast, shows a sustained commitment to regular and reserve personnel for the CF over the next two decades. Its contents stand as one legacy of the Defence Policy Statement put forward by Hillier, which at mid-decade reversed the previous trend toward marginalizing the CF.

Table 7-1 also reveals significant plans for spending on air, land, and sea equipment, along with infrastructure. Note in particular a vital $140 billion—29 percent of the total over two decades—for readiness. Lack of preparedness had been a major issue in the previously dysfunctional stage of the CF through the end of the 1990s. Even if the government had the inclination to pursue a policy option that involved the military, problems deriving from inadequate spare parts, maintenance, and training effectively prevented any sustained deployment. In sum, with the allocations designated in Table 7-1, Ottawa would have the *opportunity* to adopt policies that required a sustained military effort.

Assertions from the *Canada First* government report of 2008 reinforce the last point regarding means and ends: "the Afghanistan mission has demonstrated the importance of having a military that can operate far from home on a sustained basis and in a difficult environment, and that is capable of quickly adapting to evolving threats and changing conditions on the ground" (DND 2008, 14). Table 7-2 contains two paragraphs highlighted in *Canada First*. One paragraph is about projecting leadership abroad and summarizes lessons learned from the Afghanistan mission, while the other pertains to sustaining such a major operation. The first paragraph refers to a "complex mission" that requires "combat-capable units." Military readiness and appropriate equipment figure prominently, as does the concept of reconstruction. The second paragraph focuses on the significant numbers of military and civilian personnel essential to getting things done. The overall message of the table is that a substantial commitment to military personnel and equipment is needed for Canada to sustain missions such as Afghanistan, which are likely to reappear. Even the nation-building component of an overseas deployment, projected into the future, probably will entail providing security for reconstruction efforts at risk of attack.

Canadian military successes in Afghanistan and Libya also altered public awareness regarding the CF and legitimized a more balanced set of policies. Previously, the military had been ignored and even vilified by the Canadian public, with the low point reached around the time of the debacle in Somalia, with members of the CF found guilty of atrocious conduct. The Canadian military either occupied a negative position or at best stayed on the sidelines of Canadian consciousness until the events of 9/11. Canada then took on a combat role against the Taliban in Afghanistan. As a result of the outstanding performance of the CF, most notably in Kandahar, things began to change in Canadian society regarding the place of the military.

While resistant to the notion that Afghanistan would entail casualties, the public supported both Grit and Tory governments as the CF played significant roles in combat *and* reconstruction. The theme of balance comes to the forefront here. Canadians saw that a well-trained and properly equipped military would be necessary to meet the challenges

Table 7-2   Selected Paragraphs from *Canada First*

Projecting Leadership Abroad: Lessons Learned from the Afghanistan Mission	The Canadian Forces have learned many lessons from their complex mission in Afghanistan, and will continue to incorporate those lessons into their operational planning and training. Among other things, the Afghanistan mission has reinforced the need to: • maintain combat-capable units at the right level of readiness; • provide deployed personnel with the right mix of equipment so they can take part, on their own or with allies, in the full spectrum of operations—from countering asymmetric threats like improvised explosive devices, to contributing to reconstruction efforts in a harsh and unforgiving environment; and • work closely and develop a coherent overarching strategy with departmental partners.
Sustaining a Major Operation	Maintaining 2,500 Canadian Forces personnel in Afghanistan requires a pool of over 12,500. This includes 2,500 personnel in theatre for six months, 5,000 at different stages of training for upcoming rotations and 5,000 recovering following their deployment, affording the soldiers a minimum of 12 months between deployments. About 10,000 additional civilian and military personnel are required in Canada to support the mission.

Source: Adapted from DND 2008, 9, 15

of the new millennium, which included deployment to places such as Afghanistan, where the government simply had failed to look after its people while simultaneously promoting international terrorism. The fact that Canada sustained a military presence in Afghanistan for a decade, even allowing for a temporarily reduced role on account of inadequate capabilities, speaks volumes about the magnitude of change in the national mindset. A Canadian public that gave at least minimal consent to such a long commitment, with a direct combat role for the CF, would have been unthinkable before 9/11.

Related to the newly activated role played by the CF are significant changes that took place in security integration with the US. In the world after 9/11, border security came to the forefront in Washington, with obvious major implications for Ottawa. Given the enormous importance of the US to the Canadian economy, keeping the border open became imperative for Ottawa. Thus a wide range of previously summarized measures regarding security integration fell into place. Even by 2004, observers discerned the trend toward interoperability of the Canadian and US militaries (Welsh 2004, 76). The Tri-Command, for instance, represents yet another blended institution in the domain of security.

With regard to the long-term impact of 9/11 and subsequent security integration, consider the Beyond the Border initiative from February 2011. The supporting document's subtitle includes the words "a shared vision for perimeter security and economic competitiveness" (Canada and the US 2011). The whole idea of a *perimeter* practically speaks for itself as a quantum leap in the direction of security integration for the US and Canada. The reference to competitiveness is equally weighty; it serves as a reminder that security integration is moving forward out of perceived economic necessity for Canada as well as the need to meet the threat of terrorism.

December 2011 witnessed the release of the action plan for the Beyond the Border initiative. The highly specific plan creates substantial momentum for the process of security integration with the US. Four areas are identified as priorities for cooperation: "addressing threats early; trade facilitation, economic growth, and jobs; cross-border law enforcement; and critical infrastructure and cyber security" (Canada and the US 2011, 1). The document also creates an Executive Steering Committee to "oversee the successful implementation of the Action Plan and maintain transparency and accountability," with a meeting scheduled for 30 June 2012 and a report due by 31 December 2012 (Canada and the US 2011, 27). Taken together, the vast range of contents and a committee charged with implementation convey the seriousness of the action plan as a conduit to security integration.

Consider the contents of Table 7-3, which shows in detail how the action plan will address threats early—one of its four stipulated priorities. The table elaborates a set of goals with regard to early assessment of threats, with steps to follow and means for measuring progress made explicit in each instance. The breadth and depth of security integration conveyed by this table is striking. First, note the range of activities covered in terms of sharing research and intelligence and jointly deploying new technology, with air, land, and sea components. Second, in each of the four areas, specific next steps are designated for the two governments to take. Third, dates are listed for when to measure progress. Fourth, a number of government entities on both sides of the border are designated to carry out joint activities and assess progress. Fifth, identification and presumed elimination of "redundancies" is called for to improve shared understanding of the threat environment. In reflecting on this list, it would be difficult to imagine, prior to 9/11 and its decade of aftermath, the range, intensity, and specificity of security integration regarding early assessment of threats as mapped out by Table 7-3. A review of the other three priorities from the action plan simply would reinforce that conclusion.

Counter to the conversation so far is the *conflict* that escalated with the US in the Arctic. While cooperation with the US proceeded apace in other areas, Canadian assertiveness regarding Arctic sovereignty increased throughout the decade. Moreover, Canadian words and deeds focused primarily on perceived *US* encroachments. Especially in the most recent years, the building of infrastructure and carrying out of military exercises took place with the explicit purpose of reminding Washington that Ottawa did not welcome transit through the North without prior consent.

This shift in policy on the Arctic carried with it some irony. For many years the US had chastised Canada for its lack of resource commitment as a military ally. However, once Canada contributed effectively to Afghanistan and began to spend significant amounts of money on the CF, a more militarized response regarding Arctic sovereignty came about as a by-product. While the US military still dwarfed that of Canada in both size and state-of-the-art weaponry, the new commitment from Ottawa brought with it the means to defend sovereignty in a previously unavailable way. Since standing up to Washington on Arctic sovereignty possesses appeal across the Canadian political spectrum, it is not surprising to see the prime minister playing that recently available card on a regular basis.

Difficult to miss in the last decade is the shocking decline of NATO as an instrument for security policy. As Canada became more assertive

Table 7-3   Addressing Threats Early

Goals	Next Steps and Measuring Progress
Enhance our shared understanding of the threat environment through joint, integrated threat assessments, improving our intelligence and national security information sharing	Next Steps: A bilateral group of senior government leaders with intelligence and public safety responsibilities will survey existing intelligence work to identify redundancies and gaps to develop a framework to guide the selection of joint projects. The framework will leverage existing forums, emphasize the need to economize resources, and establish performance metrics. Measuring Progress: The US Office of the Director of National Intelligence, the US Department of Homeland Security (DHS), and Public Safety Canada, in coordination with relevant intelligence agencies in both countries, will produce a joint inventory of existing work and a gap analysis and identify next steps by September 30, 2012.
Share information and intelligence in support of law enforcement and national security	Next Steps: We will improve information sharing while respecting each country's respective constitutional and legal frameworks, including the following areas of work: • addressing agency policies that may improve information sharing, including by developing clear channels or mechanisms for cross-border sharing of intelligence and information; • promoting increased informal sharing of law enforcement intelligence, information, and evidence through police and prosecutorial channels consistent with the respective domestic laws of each country; and • examining whether current frameworks should be changed to address impediments to cooperation, and to ensure that the terms of applicable laws, agreements and treaties provide the widest measure of cooperation possible. We will utilize the Cross-Border Crime Forum and create other forums to discuss ways to improve law enforcement information sharing practices, and to identify opportunities to improve effective and responsible national security intelligence information sharing. Measuring Progress: By January 31, 2012, the US Department of Justice, DHS, Public Safety Canada, and Justice Canada will determine the way ahead.

Table 7-3   continued

Enhance domain awareness in the air, land, and maritime environments	Next Steps: We will develop and implement processes, procedures, and policies to enable an effective, shared understanding of activities, threats, and criminal trends or other consequences in the air, land, and maritime environments. This will be achieved through intelligence analysis, effective and timely information sharing, a common understanding of the environment, and an inventory of current capabilities. We will • create an inventory of American and Canadian domain awareness capabilities at the border by May 31, 2012, and identify gaps and vulnerabilities in capabilities by October 31, 2012; • prioritize coverage of gaps by April 30, 2013, to create a vision for jointly deploying new technology to address identified gaps; and • establish a process by April 30, 2013, to coordinate the joint procurement and deployment of technology along the border. Measuring Progress: DHS, the Royal Canadian Mounted Police (RCMP), and Transport Canada will report on progress toward achieving this work by the timelines indicated above.
Cooperate to counter violent extremism in our two countries	Next Steps: We will • coordinate and share research on how people become radicalized and turn to violence; • share best practices and tools for law enforcement and corrections partners to detect, prevent, and respond to this threat; • develop a common messaging and strategic communications approach; and • emphasize community-based and community-driven efforts. This will include collaborating on how to engage with communities and build their resilience against violent extremists who seek to target specific communities in our respective countries, as well as coordinating community outreach. Measuring Progress: Progress updates will be provided to the US Secretary of Homeland Security and Canada Minister of Public Safety on a semi-annual basis.

Source: Adapted from Canada and the US 2011, 3–4

in carrying out its security policy, the principal alliance to which it belonged went into disarray. Previously, Canada had been targeted by the US in particular as a free rider on the efforts of other governments when it came to providing security. Ottawa had insisted on an exclusively peacekeeping mission for the CF and received criticism from its allies, especially the US, in return. The role played by the CF in Kandahar put all of that in reverse. As the CF carried out its mission in an increasingly autonomous and effective manner, the military deployments from most other NATO governments embarrassed themselves through a virtual unwillingness to take any risks at all. The CF fought intense military engagements in Kandahar while troops from supposedly greater powers, such as Germany, hid behind caveats and played no significant role beyond reconstruction.

Fast-forward by a few years and the pattern in Libya is the same: only eight NATO members, including Canada, took part in bombing missions, and two governments, Germany and Poland, stayed out of the fight. Table 7-4 conveys the essentials from Operation Mobile, Canada's military response to the Libyan civil strife during 2011. The 1,539 sorties from the air force over the course of the mission reflect new capability and willingness on the part of government and society to take action on behalf of Canadian values. Unlike Afghanistan, Libya did not pose a terrorist threat, but its people faced suppression by a brutal dictator when they attempted to speak out against his long and tyrannical rule. The air war fought by Canada over the skies of Libya reflected a new Canada: one with an ability and an inclination to use realist means toward liberal ends.

Continuity also is evident in Canadian government and society, in spite of the major, even transforming, changes summarized here. Notable instances include features related to the War in Afghanistan, refusal of the Iraq War, the long process of decision making and ultimately negative verdict on BMD, and a point of qualification embedded in the extensive agenda of the action plan for the Beyond the Border initiative.

Table 7-4   Operation Mobile Sorties[a]

Type of Aircraft	Number of Sorties[b]
CF-188 Hornet fighters	946
CC-150 Polaris tankers	250
CP-140 Aurora long-range patrol aircraft	181
CC-130J Hercules airlifters	23
CC-130 Hercules tankers[c]	139
All types of aircraft combined	1,539

Source: Adapted from DFAIT 2011a

[a]This is the final estimated total as of 5:30 a.m. Greenwich Mean Time, 28 October 2011.

[b]A sortie, as defined by NATO, is an operational flight by one aircraft.

[c]In September 2011 the CF redeployed these aircraft to Canada.

Canada played a combat role in Afghanistan, which constituted a major departure from the status quo. This deployment occurred, however, with established values playing a visible role. Canadian entry into the war provoked limited controversy at home because of its multilateral and legitimized character. Both the UN and NATO had approved of collective military action against the Taliban as a sponsor of international terrorism carried out by al Qaeda. In addition, the Canadian government insisted on passing legislation that authorized a more vigilant security policy at home and abroad.

Moreover, interviews with members of the CF show anything but a disposition toward conquest in carrying out their duties in Afghanistan. What comes through instead is a commitment to the interlocking values of democracy, freedom, and human rights. Canadian soldiers justified the resort to arms in those terms.

With time it became obvious that both liberal values regarding human security and realist principles about the exercise of power had to co-exist in any effective policy for turning around a difficult situation such as Afghanistan. Reconstruction, an activity consistent with liberalism, would have to take place in equal measure with counter-insurgency, a task more in line with realism. Thus Afghanistan revealed important points of continuity with a human security agenda even as combat raged on.

Canada did not move in lockstep when the US followed up on Afghanistan with an attempt to oust Saddam Hussein. Canada refused to join in the Iraq War in spite of considerable US interest in at least tacit approval from Ottawa. The most basic reason behind that decision rests with the established value both the government and society placed on multilateralism and legitimacy obtained through international institutions. Unlike the War in Afghanistan, which had UN and NATO stamps of approval, the Iraq conflict seemed more like the stereotypical John Wayne version of the US—using force and going it alone—so the venture lacked appeal north of the border. From the viewpoint of most Canadians, the Coalition of the Willing looked like a fig leaf for American unilateralism and disposition toward military solutions.

BMD's gradual playing out as an issue, along with its negative outcome, showcases the skeptical side of Canadian culture vis-à-vis weapons in general and ongoing reluctance about security integration. A weapons system promoted by respective US leaders as defensive in nature and freely available failed to produce a favourable response from Canada. Instead, public support oscillated and ultimately drifted downward as BMD became a casualty of the Iraq War, which had made the purveyor of the idea, President George W. Bush, *persona non grata* among most of Canadian society. Stereotypically aggressive behaviour by the president while visiting Canada pushed the prime minister over the edge and precipitated rejection of missile defence.

One awkward point about the way in which refusal of BMD ultimately took place is that it reflects another long-established Canadian value: anti-Americanism. The record is clear that continuing the dialogue on missile defence would have been in the national interest, but instead the prime minister opted for outright refusal. Even skeptics about BMD have observed that continuing the wait-and-see approach would have been a preferred tactic, given US sensitivity about security issues just a few years after 9/11. However, when publicly backed into a corner, the prime minister had to think first about political survival. He naturally rode the rising tide of sentiment against the US and rejected the offer to participate in BMD.

Greatly enhanced security integration would appear to be an open-and-shut instance of change, but an important element of continuity appears in the action plan for the Beyond the Border initiative reviewed earlier. In Table 7-3, which conveys further planned steps for addressing threats early, a notable qualification appears. Information sharing will be improved "while respecting each country's respective constitutional and legal frameworks" (Canada and the US 2011, 3–4). This point is in line with legislation passed by Canada in the immediate aftermath of 9/11 to ensure that security measures would take place within constitutional limits. The action plan for security integration thereby shows the persistence of the rule of law as a Canadian value even in the most urgent domain of national security policy.

While aspects of continuity are plain to see, the answer to the question of change is summed up in one word: *transformation*. The reason is that the *means* of security policy changed in kind, not just degree. At both psychological and material levels, the position of the military had changed. Witness the Canadian roles in Afghanistan and Libya, which involved combat action. This contrasts with the previous commitment to peacekeeping as the CF's basic purpose. A quantum leap also occurred in security coordination with the US. The institutional buildup of the preceding decade is noteworthy in terms of both breadth and depth.

With regard to *ends*, change also took place, but more as a matter of degree than in kind. Canada showed its new realist side most directly in the Arctic, where it confronted US encroachments and engaged in military deployments to demonstrate a commitment to sovereignty.

Taken together, means and ends changed significantly over the years since 9/11 vis-à-vis Canadian security policy. While obviously it could be argued back and forth whether *transformation* is the right word to sum all this up, the change clearly is qualitative rather than strictly quantitative. Canadian security policy looks fundamentally different today than it did before 9/11.

Do Canadians Have an Accurate Sense of Their Place on the International Stage?

Canada's role in the world in the post–World War II era up to 9/11 can be summed up most accurately as a "middle power."[1] This identity started out with a commitment to promotion of democracy and peace, development assistance, and multilateralism. Put simply, Canada identified strongly with the values articulated by the UN at the time of its founding and it still does. With time, the peacekeeping element of the middle-power role came to the fore. All of this made sense for a peaceful and prosperous nation that had an interest in bringing order to a troubled world—a status quo–oriented power, in the language of realism—and the Nobel Prize won by Lester Pearson for his diplomacy during the Suez crisis and war became the signature event in constructing Canadian identity. Thus Canadian self-identification as a middle power became solidified over decades and seemed firmly in place by the end of the millennium.

With time, however, the role played by Canada on the world stage seemed out of kilter with self-perception. For example, over the course of decades, an active role in peacekeeping held pride of place in the Canadian identity as a middle power that promoted a better world for all. By the eve of 9/11, however, Canada no longer did much peacekeeping. Its development assistance could be found wanting as well; while CIDA provided aid to a wide range of destinations, experiences in Afghanistan soon would highlight serious problems with effectiveness.

One prominent critic summed up Canadian foreign policy in the following way (Hart 2008, 273):

> Much of Canada's activity around the world can be described as the diplomacy of humanitarian gestures (e.g., foreign aid or disaster relief), of paying global dues (e.g., sending peacekeepers to places most Canadians would have trouble finding on a map), of maintaining club membership (e.g., representation at various regional banks), of building relations for future contingencies (Canadian embassies in middle-level countries), of responding to the pride of ethnic communities (e.g., some of Canada's smaller embassies abroad in places such as Latvia and Sri Lanka) or of responding to the needs of Canadians travelling abroad. Little of this activity, however, is easily related to fundamental Canadian interests.

Hart (2008, 97, 24, 25), to continue, regarded this package of activities as "vapid internationalism and drift," with the emphasis on projecting Canadian values abroad leading to "unhelpful self-congratulation" and even "smugness." It would be difficult to imagine a more scathing critique of a government which, after all, had not engaged in aggression against others.

While at least some of the preceding critique might apply to the Canada that existed prior to 9/11, the publication date of 2008 makes the assertions puzzling. By the middle of the last decade, Canada had shifted to a highly responsible role as a NATO ally in carrying out combat and reconstruction activities in Afghanistan. Perhaps the strong statements from Hart are more appropriate for the situation a few years earlier, in which words largely had replaced deeds when it came to security policy writ large. Both fighting and nation-building capacities had eroded to near non-existence in a Canada that had put its financial house in order but, as a by-product, favoured rhetoric over action in engaging with the outside world. In a phrase, talk is cheap.

With the perspective available from a full decade of hindsight, Canada at 9/11 appears out of balance. It had tilted so far toward the liberal end of the continuum that it is virtually impossible to find acknowledgement of a realist point of view. The latter outlook would turn out to have renewed relevance when al Qaeda shocked the world on 9/11. Canada would have to adapt to a setting in which some highly relevant participants insisted on pursuit of violence to achieve their ends; no amount of rhetoric or goodwill could make that go away.

Canadians today, as a result of experiences over the last 10 years, seem more in balance and accurate about their country's role on the world stage. While Ottawa cooperated with Washington in the war against Afghanistan and the intervention in Libya, along with border security, it pushed back on demands that seemed to violate core values. Efforts to protect Arctic sovereignty, coupled with the rejection of the Iraq War and BMD, show Canada preserving its distance from the US. The mixture of these policy outcomes could be described as what would be expected from a pragmatic balance between liberal and realist points of view.

Is Canada Performing Well in Terms of Decision Making, and In What Ways Can It Do Better?

While a response to this question could touch on many challenges, a basic problem stands out: the tendency of domestic politics to intrude into decision making about security policy in potentially harmful ways. Since the Cold War era, democracies, collectively speaking, have become more prone to partisan politics (Hart 2008, 7). Canada is no exception. For Ottawa the problem is manifested in the distorting role played by anti-Americanism, which has deep origins in Canadian history. Challenging as well is a tendency toward moral superiority among the Canadian public as a by-product of ongoing comparison with the US.

Long known is the tendency for Canadians to stress and even exaggerate how Canada is different from the US (Thompson and Randall 2008, 337; Biette 2008, 388).[2] Perhaps this is precisely because the range of similarities is vast. Both Canada and the US are multicultural settler societies built on an Aboriginal base. Each is democratic and federal, with a prosperous market economy. Both are under mostly common law, with specified individual rights and freedoms and limitations on the role of government (Hart 2008, 207, 213–14; Thompson and Randall 2008, 336–37; Biette 2008, 388). A much longer list could be supplied, but the preceding items should be sufficient to make the point regarding common traits.

Canadian efforts to appear different would appear, therefore, to be motivated at least in part by anti-Americanism (Hart 2008, 31). For example, policy under Chrétien seemed to emphasize preserving distance from the US more than any clear Canadian interests—the "worst prescription" according Allan Gotlieb, a former Canadian ambassador to Washington (2004, 28, 31). Consider the words of former cabinet minister John Manley: "We should differ from the Americans when we think they're wrong *and we shouldn't feel that somehow our identity is challenged when we agree with them when they're right*" (quoted in Chapnick 2002, 347).[3] In sum, insecurity is a poor guide to policy.

Anti-Americanism is an enduring theme. It is identified regularly as a problem by those commenting on Canadian politics and policy. To some degree the disposition is understandable because the two neighbours, after all, "exist in a relationship of unequal co-dependency" (Chapnick 2002, 348). The long-standing US doctrine of manifest destiny, for example, is unpleasant for Canada because it contributes to a sense of "vulnerability and fear" (Dyment 2010, 113). With its overwhelming power, the US even seems at times to be a rampaging elephant from the Canadian point of view. Thus agreements with Washington "tend to be seen through a highly suspicious lens on the home front" (Burney 2005, 14). Sovereignty and even preservation of an independent government and way of life can be aroused as issues among the Canadian public in response to even relatively mild clumsiness from the neighbour to the south.

Anti-Americanism, at its worst, is "ignorant, small-minded, and often driven by fear and envy" (Hart 2008, 31). For such reasons, anti-Americanism can play a corrosive role in moving Canadians away from pursuit of their national interests (Hart 2008, 100). Critics of the Chrétien era of foreign policy, for example, saw its rejection of partnership with the US as a product of "mercurial whims and populist instincts" (Hart 2008, 89). Note that such criticism is not necessarily destined to become partisan; the Liberal Pearson government, by contrast, maintained good relations with the US, while the Conservative Diefenbaker government did not. Instead, regardless of party affiliation, the temptation for Canadian politicians to attack the US as a means of rallying support at home always exists. This tactic may produce the desired end inside Canada, but it can distort security policy at the same time.

Consider the issues of Iraq and BMD from the last decade. Regardless of their content, these decisions are unflattering to Canada in terms of *style*. In both instances Canada said "no" on issues that appeared to be important to the US. With the perspective offered by time, and to some degree even as events unfolded, it is clear that the decisions themselves did not cause problems with Washington. Instead, in each case, the prime ministers—Chrétien and Martin, respectively—seemed from a US point of view to go out of their way to refuse US overtures with a flourish. The lack of courtesy on these occasions, even in the context of serious policy disagreement, is difficult to explain in any way other than as an attempt to exploit the underlying reservoir of anti-Americanism for political gain. Critics from across the political spectrum have reiterated that conclusion.

Some reflections on Canadian engagement with the world are unflattering at a more encompassing level. The problem is not just anti-Americanism but perhaps also a tendency toward narcissism. "The debate," according to a pointed exposition on foreign policy (Hart 2008, 3), "is all about how Canadians *feel* about themselves and how they want others to *perceive* them." Unfortunately, feeling good about oneself "is not the same as doing good for others" (Hart 2008, 203). Oddly enough, words taken from a government report convey about the same message: the Canadian "self-image as a moral nation is built more on the way we treat ourselves—through programs such as national health care—than on the way we treat others" (Canada 2006b, 27). In particular, "to suggest that Canadian foreign policy should be characterized as a truth required to speak to the abuse of power by the United States and other major players is both offensive and morally cloying" (Hart 2008, 305). Another critic sums up the situation as follows: a "detached, somewhat sentimental attitude about our place in the world is not preparing us for the complexities of globalization or the threats to our economic well being" (Burney 2005, 15–16). From these observations come a sense of Canadians making decisions based more on internal needs than external conditions.

These criticisms look increasingly dated. Much of what appears could apply to the Canada that existed before 9/11. Consider the situation just before the terror attacks of that day: While the CF supposedly existed to perform peacekeeping, not much of it took place any more. Canada *did* take a leading role in the treaty to ban land mines, but even there it would be possible to see excesses regarding presumed moral superiority over others. Most extreme, perhaps, would be Axworthy's high-profile designation of Canada as a moral superpower. With arguably the world's leading resource endowment and the US providing for virtually all security needs, Canada in the eyes of the rest of the world might have appeared more fortunate than virtuous.

Canada today looks more worldly and engaged than it did a decade ago. Both government and society are in touch with the need to act pragmatically in a world with many dangers; both liberal and realist means may be required to protect long-standing values that include democracy, freedom, and human rights. How, then, might decision making be improved in the future? Key priorities include pursuit of national interests and making the best of things with the US.

What is meant by the national interest? It is a concept that stands above how Canada relates to the US or any other entity. Interests need to be assessed and acted on (Dyment 2010, 81). As articulated by a government document titled *Managing Turmoil*, "Canada is a sovereign nation and acts in its own interests. Those interests coincide with the United States in many matters. When they do not, Canada should pursue its own interests" (Canada 2006b, 35). *Managing Turmoil* urged a pragmatic working relationship with the US because enhancement of security and economic well-being for Canadians also strengthens sovereignty (Canada 2006b, 38; see also Dyment 2010, 47).

Canadians could move in the right direction by learning more about Americans, their principal partners in the realm of security and so many other things. It is true already that Canadians pay much more attention to what the US is doing than vice versa (Goldenberg 2006, 299; Hart 2008, 246). However, Canadians do not understand the US very well—certainly not at the level of comprehension that people credit to themselves (Welsh 2004, 51; Dyment 2010, 40–41). The US is not a rogue superpower but instead a "problem-solver" with a short- rather than long-term focus (Welsh 2004, 52, 53). Domestic politics rather than sinister intentions, as it turns out, are more helpful in accounting for US policies.

Poorly grasped in particular is the US political system. Canadians put too much emphasis on how the prime minister and president of the day might be getting along. Greatly underrated in the Canadian mindset are the bureaucracy and legislature south of the border. Both of these entities lack cohesion yet exert great influence (Goldenberg 2006, 301; Hart 2008, 242; Dyment 2010, 42, 44, 45). The US system of government most assuredly is *not* parliamentary. Instead, it is based on separation of powers and this becomes a major force in shaping foreign as well as domestic policy. The near permanent electoral cycle in the US is confusing to Canadians, who are used to Cabinet solidarity and party discipline under a prime minister.

One side effect of this misunderstanding is a Canadian tendency to project thought processes onto Americans that simply are not present. In particular, the Canadian media attributes motives to Washington that it does not possess, as pointed out by one prominent observer from the centre-left of the political spectrum (Goldenberg 2006, 390). If anything, the pernicious role of domestic politics, especially on Capitol Hill, should be accepted as creating a difficult and sometimes impossible set of constraints for even the most well-intentioned president.

Experiences with the US serve as a reminder that Canada should identify and act on its *interests*. Canada competes with many other governments for US attention and that naturally works toward the advantage of Washington over Ottawa (Dyment 2010, 75). In particular, advancing the national interest "can and must be separated from either anti-Americanism or being a vassal state" (Dyment 2010, 81, 86). Canada needs, in short, to return to basics; ignoring national interests is utopianism and Canadians need to identify their goals and the tools required to meet them (Hart 2008, ix, 129, 335; see also Hillier 2010, 155; Welsh 2004, 20, 23).

Shared experiences in Afghanistan may affect relations for Canada and the US over many years to come. Each contributed effectively, in contrast to certain other NATO allies, to both reconstruction and fighting against the insurgency. This positive experience helps to counteract US notions of Canada as weak and irresponsible regarding matters of security. Thus, with respect to the US and the world in general, Canada can make better decisions by sustaining the new emphasis on balancing liberal and realist means toward accomplishing its security-related national interests.

In What Ways Is Canada Unique?

Canada has emerged from its trials and tribulations of the last decade as a possibly unique player in world politics. The pendulum metaphor is helpful here. Previous chapters have referred to Canadian security policy, in connection with overall identity, as being very far in the direction of liberalism and human security prior to 9/11. After that cataclysmic day, the world witnessed a Canadian pendulum swinging back toward realism and national security. As the earlier review of points of continuity reveals, however, Canada has not abandoned its previously established values. Instead, contemporary security policy embraces a *balance* between liberalism and realism regarding means and ends.

While involved in more warfare over the last decade than it had been in the prior half-century, Canada did not engage in conquest. Instead, reflections from leaders and citizens alike include concerns about making life better for people in places where Canada had intervened. The Canadian pendulum, it might be said, is centred in a way that may be unique around the world when it comes to balancing liberalism and realism in the means and ends of security policy.

What Is Canada's Likely Future Direction in Security Policy?

This final question will be answered through further application of the pendulum metaphor. Once again, imagine liberalism and realism at opposite extremes for such a pendulum when it swings. The query about the likely direction of Canada now can be answered in three basic ways: swinging toward one of the extremes of realism or liberalism, or more limited movement around the centre. All of these possibilities are considered in turn.

What about the possibility that Canada, in response to so many challenges, will swing toward the extreme of realism? Canada certainly exists in a world of many dangers that could encourage a mindset in favour of relative gains and military means toward such ends. Consider a summary from a government committee of the challenges facing Canada: Islamic jihad, religious radicalism, expansion of nuclear weapons, states versus non-states, decline of UN, decline of NATO, rich versus poor, world energy supplies, world water supplies, deterioration of environment, globalization, rise of Asia's economy, US debt, US world involvement, and Canadian military spending (Canada 2006b, 17–23). More items easily could be added to the list.

From data presented earlier in this chapter, it is obvious that Canada now is more open, at least in principle, to use of military means to achieve desired ends. A possible danger of this shift is progression toward a "garrison state," an ominous-sounding term from one of the classic expositions on political sociology (Lasswell 1941). The basic idea of the garrison state is that a government can fall under the control of a military specialist, who in turn begins to shift foreign policy and even alters society across the board—put simply, realism gone mad. Is Canada in any danger of such a fate?

While he does not go that far, Harvey's (2007, 284) concept of the "homeland security dilemma" points toward a parallel type of danger for Canada in the world after 9/11: "enormous investments in security inevitably raise public expectations and amplify public outrage after subsequent failure." Harvey sees the pre-eminent position of security on Washington's agenda as having "obvious and disturbing" implications for Ottawa; no matter what amount of effort Canada might make toward enhanced security, even a hint of danger from north of its border would be sufficient to trigger further demands from the US (Harvey 2007, 309, 310). Thus pressure from the US to engage in further spending and security integration could be expected, making a Canadian drift toward the garrison state not beyond the realm of possibility.

While the US undoubtedly will continue to exert influence on Canada, worries about an ultra-realist Canada seem misplaced. The underlying cultural consensus in favour of democracy, the rule of law, and human rights is quite entrenched. So, too, is a disposition against a martial culture. Furthermore, Afghanistan and Libya, the most recent instances of combat, unfolded in ways that *affirmed* underlying Canadian values in opposition to a culture of militarism and conquest.

What about a swing of the pendulum in the opposite direction? This would constitute, in effect, a return to the ultra-liberalism of the 1990s. Limited results, however, are likely to accrue from a resurrection of strictly liberal means and ends. As one commentator on Canadian security policy observed, "putting all of our eggs in the UN basket isn't sufficient" (Welsh 2004, 20). While liberal ends still might predominate, a wider range of means will be required to meet the challenges of today's world. This refers, in particular, to an active role for the military. Positive effects from Canadian military action in Afghanistan and Libya demonstrate that point most directly. Some problems simply cannot be resolved by the UN, but Canada still can try to meet those challenges by coordinating with various combinations of other governments and international organizations that seek to promote democracy, human rights, and the rule of law.

Liberalism in its purest form may be ruled out of hand because of the degree of security integration in place with the US. While nothing like the EU appears to be on the horizon, the widening and deepening of security institutions likely will create a ratchet effect. Canadian refusal to cooperate on efforts toward mutual security might be a moot point because the degree of integration is so extensive already. Put differently, the rise of the

CF and many steps in the direction of security integration with the US make Canada unlikely to swing back dramatically toward liberalism.

Balance in security policy—a hybrid of liberalism and realism in means and ends—is by far the most likely outcome for the foreseeable future. The Canadian pendulum is likely to swing in a limited way back and forth between liberalism and realism, as opposed to the huge displacement seen over the last two decades in both directions. This prediction makes sense because balance will tend to produce the best outcomes, on average, and thereby build support in government and society for more of the same basic approach.

What, then, does a balanced security policy mean in practice? A full answer to that query is beyond the scope of this book, but the basic idea is not difficult to convey. Liberalism and realism should be combined pragmatically to further Canada's national interests.

Canada, on the liberal side, might aim to become a "model citizen" for the twenty-first century (Welsh 2004, 187–88). This would involve a firm commitment to furthering the most basic Canadian values: democracy, the rule of law, and human rights (Welsh 2004, 207). On the realist side, Canada could return to functionalism of the kind practised by Prime Minister Mackenzie King, getting involved and seeking to have an impact on specific issues where realistic (Gotlieb 2004, 41). Consider peacekeeping as an example: "selective, prudent and meaningful participation in UN operations could serve a useful purpose—both in broader humanitarian and geopolitical terms and in terms of Canada's own national interest" (Shadwick 2006, 95). Note that means and ends become symbiotic here; Canada would use whatever works in a given context to further its interests, which are based on enduring values.

Some final words are in order. This book started out with a set of questions about Canada in conflict. The straightforward answer to the most general query about change is that the years since 9/11 have transformed Canada—and almost certainly for the better. The Canada of today is more balanced in its engagement with the rest of the world. Its pragmatic combination of liberal and realist means and ends is a model for the effective practice of security policy.

Notes

Chapter 1

1. As observed by former prime minister Paul Martin in his memoirs (2008, 371), Canadians tend to link security issues to underlying problems arising from development. While well-understood and convincing, it is not possible to take this point of view fully into account. Only a more panoramic study that traces the origins and traits of Canadian security policies to either democratic deficits or poverty around the world could meet that requirement.
2. The most recent figures available on Canadian trade and investment, which convey the expansive role of the US, appear in Canada (2011c).
3. Specialists in international relations will recognize the notion of a filter as the "attitudinal prism" from the classic exposition of foreign policy analysis provided by Brecher (1972).

Chapter 2

1. Pigott (2007, 79) summarizes Canada's limited involvement in Afghanistan prior to 9/11: CF personnel served in Afghanistan, 1985–91; land mine detection; CDN$123 million in humanitarian assistance and food aid, 1990–2001; CIDA's Kabul Widow's Feeding project, 1988–89.
2. The impact of this substantial reduction could be seen in various ways even in the new millennium: "Canadian reservists on exercise were regularly denied ammunition, with enough of them crying 'Bang! Bang!' when they 'fired' a shot that the term 'militia bullets' was coined" (Blatchford 2008, 38–39).
3. Prior to 9/11, according to one observer, the CF "usually acted as though applicants ought to be grateful if they were even given a look," with a "top speed [that] tended toward the glacial" (Blatchford 2008, 8).
4. At the end of 2002, Canada ranked thirty-fourth in the number of troops allocated to UN-sponsored peacekeeping (Richter 2006, 70).
5. Canadians took pride in the success of Lester B. Pearson, who in the role of foreign minister brokered a peace during the Suez war of 1956. The concept of peacekeeping is identified closely with Pearson, who won a Nobel Peace Prize and went on to become prime minister in the 1960s (Bothwell 2006, 384; Gotlieb 2004, 10). Pearson, however, may have been acting more out of Canadian interest in maintaining good relations among allies than a straightforward concern for peace in the Middle East (Hart 2008, 275; see also Shadwick 2006, 95). This suggests that his legacy is mixed: not purely liberal but also realist to at least some degree.
6. One especially forbidding region north of Kandahar City, the Shah Wali-Kot, earned the nickname *Middle-earth* (i.e., from J.R.R. Tolkien's fantasy novels) among the CF (Windsor, Charters, and Wilson 2008, 32).
7. Known formally as the Independent Panel on Canada's Future Role in Afghanistan, and informally as the Manley Report, this document is cited as the Independent Panel (2008).
8. Details provided in this chapter regarding 9/11 are those that pertain most directly to Canada's reaction in the context of the Afghan war. Other aspects that

focus more directly on Can/Am security issues aside from Afghanistan are included in Chapter 5.

9. Easily overlooked because battles in Afghanistan took place on land, the Canadian naval commitment to Operation Apollo included six warships and 1,500 personnel (Granatstein and Oliver 2011, 4).

10. The prime minister showed particular sensitivity to US concerns by asking John Manley to take responsibility for border issues because he had not tried in the past to "score points at home" via anti-Americanism (Goldenberg 2006, 266). The theme of anti-Americanism is pursued at greater length in Chapter 7.

11. Dey (2011) refers to this as the "liberal" explanation for why Canada went to war, but that term is used differently in this study. Liberal accounts, as referenced here, pertain to the role of institutions in bringing about international cooperation. The government and domestic politics in the present study is the school of thought identified with what Dey labels the "liberal" point of view.

Chapter 3

1. The specific contributions of Canadian PRT work will be reviewed in this chapter's section on the consequences of involvement.

2. While Ottawa did not impose caveats, the military certainly did. In Kabul during 2004–5, the CF operated with severe restrictions that changed only with Hillier becoming CDS in 2005 (Saideman and Auerswald 2012).

3. In his autobiography, former president George W. Bush (2010, 212) emphasizes the full-fledged fighting role played by Canada in Afghanistan. Great Britain is the only other major state mentioned favourably in the stage of his discussion focusing on NATO in Afghanistan.

4. A study of Canada, France, and Germany identifies two factors as essential in accounting for national caveats: political institutions and individual leaders (Saideman and Auerswald 2012). With regard to the role of individual leaders, prior personal experience tells the story. For example, Germany, with a leadership greatly concerned from the outset about casualties and inhibitions about the deportment of its soldiers as a result of World War II, stood at one end of the continuum. Canada, with less "baggage," showed more of a focus, especially in the Hillier era of leadership, on managing rather than avoiding risk (Saideman and Auerswald 2012).

5. For the other side of the argument, which criticizes the impatience of both Martin and many of his supporters, see Goldenberg (2006).

6. From Arabic, *shura* "roughly translates as 'consultation,' but the word's lexical meaning—'to get the honey out of its sources'—far better captures the leisurely pace of the process" (Blatchford 2008, 100).

7. The CF came in and out of various operations held under the auspices of OEF and ISAF. For example, CF once again participated in Operation Athena during its consolidation and closeout phases of 2011. No attempt will be made in the present account to cover the full details of these complex deployments.

8. With a graduate degree from the University of Calgary, Harper is identified with an ideology of conservatism based at that institution. Known as the Calgary School, prominent academics from that university advocate political and social conservatism, with an implicitly positive disposition toward the military as an institution within society. See James (2010) for an extensive treatment of the Calgary School as a force within the academic study of Canadian politics.

9. Blatchford (2008, 129), however, reports both positive and negative sides to the reaction among Canadians: "Suddenly a couple of things seemed to come clear to the back-home audience. One was that Afghanistan was a place where danger did not always arrive by conventional means but could come from any quarter at any time. The second was that whatever one's view of the mission as an expression of Canadian foreign policy, those young soldiers were pretty damn impressive."

10. Descriptions of battles involving the Taliban and the CF in the summer of 2006 are based primarily on Blatchford (2008), Wattie (2008), Windsor, Charters, and Wilson (2008), and Horn (2010).

11. IEDs, as described by Blatchford (2008, 97), "vary widely and are limited only by the bomber's ingenuity and the materials at his disposal."

12. National Defence Headquarters in Ottawa sometimes revealed a lack of understanding with respect to on-the-ground conditions, which in turn could result in absurd orders. For example, CF could not bring along enough water to carry out patrols beyond eight hours in the summer heat, yet somehow would be told do so anyway (Day 2010, 238; see also Hillier 2010, 258–59). In addition, Canadian military lawyers in one intense engagement refused to authorize a fire mission to support ground troops because nearby civilian buildings, which were deserted anyway, might be damaged (Wattie 2008, 265). Multiple lawyers intervened in mid-battle on matters related to Canadian law and national policy, along with the international laws of armed conflict, on an ongoing basis (Blatchford 2008, 255). While this reduced the likelihood of collateral damage in particular, it also added further complexity to CF missions.

13. May 2007 also brought news regarding the death of Mullah Dadullah Akhund, who had planned the attack in Kandahar the preceding August; special forces killed him in Helmand Province (Wattie 2008, 289).

Chapter 4

1. Dey (2011, 8) asserts that "one of the main problems with the *Unexpected War* (Stein and Lang 2007) is its acceptance of politicians' reflections on what happened as what *actually* happened."

2. It is possible to monitor progress on these projects and other Canadian government activities through reports from DFAIT, both quarterly and ad hoc (e.g., DFAIT 2011c, 2011e, 2011g).

3. The higher level of respect accorded by Afghans to the ANA is confirmed even earlier by the *Afghanistan Study Group Report* (CSPC 2008, 24). Nearly 90 percent of Afghans surveyed said they trusted the ANA.

4. Marijuana also serves as a major cash crop. Growing conditions create marijuana fields taller than a soldier, and CF even used the plants to camouflage huge armoured vehicles (Day 2010, 80, 98). At times the pervasive presence of the drug trade reached the level of dark comedy. During one battle, an ANP commander "had received a call from the fellow who owned the marijuana field on the north side of the wadi [i.e., valley]. The man wasn't phoning to report the forty Taliban hiding in his field, but rather to complain that they were crushing his hash" (Blatchford 2008, 18).

5. Ongoing support for the Taliban from Pashtuns in particular occurs for many reasons: "a craving for stability and order, self-interest, disillusionment with warlords, dislike of outsiders, discouragement regarding the slow pace of development, a desire to see the Pashtuns paramount in their country rather than the non-Pashtun Northern Alliance, and religious zeal" (Smith 2007, 4).

6. Caveats did exist in Kosovo but did not matter much because of the rarity of ground combat. NATO quarrels in that instance focused on targeting for the bombing campaign.
7. Some readers will recall that the Dieppe raid of 19 August 1942 evoked similar ideas. This assault on the German Atlantic defences, which involved a small force composed primarily of Canadians, achieved none of its objectives. For many years after, however, it would be remembered among many Canadians as significant to the outcome of the European campaign in World War II.

Chapter 5

1. Consider the list of problems in Canada's relationship with the US identified a few years after 9/11 by just one well-informed observer (Welsh 2004, 36–37): Camp X-Ray in Cuba regarding al Qaeda detainees; US protectionist measures against European steel and Canadian lumber; threats to veto extension of the UN peacekeeping mission in Bosnia; the US not signing major international agreements such as Kyoto and the International Criminal Court; plans for national missile defence; and especially pre-emptive defence, labelled as the Bush Doctrine.
2. Canada and the US are involved in numerous multilateral institutions and activities. Issues with dimensions beyond Can/Am relations are included, but for reasons of feasibility are referenced only in that bilateral context. For present purposes, only the Can/Am aspects of multilateral ventures, such as the Arctic Council or NATO involvement in Libya, are explored.
3. Only Afghanistan, covered already in Chapters 2, 3, and 4, would exceed the level of attention devoted to the issues just mentioned. Afghanistan will come in and out of the discussion when essential to understanding the development of these other issues.
4. The Fenian Brotherhood, composed of Irish-Americans, carried out their raids in an effort to coerce Britain into leaving Ireland. Fenian raiding petered out by the early 1870s.
5. The method used in Antarctica, a single continent, is not feasible in the Arctic. This sector-based approach, as it is known under international law, breaks down because of all the islands (Wrangel Island, Russia; Greenland; Denmark) and Alaska (US) in the Far North. In contrast to the straight territorial lines of Antarctica, the Arctic under the sector-based principle would look more like a spider web.
6. From a Canadian nationalist perspective, however, the security guarantees had unpleasant implications. For one observer these reciprocal statements symbolized Canada's transition into a "willing American protectorate" (Clarkson 2002, 382).
7. At the time of its creation, the organization was named North American Air Defence Command.
8. The overview in this paragraph is based on St. John (2011).
9. The full text is available at http://laws-lois.justice.gc.ca/eng/acts/A-12/FullText.html. Details that follow are taken directly from that text.
10. Reports at the time that the Patriot missile system had succeeded turned out later to be false. However, the symbolic value of its use as a defensive response to a missile attack had the effect of encouraging more research and development.
11. Interesting to note is that the two missile defence–oriented paragraphs in the White Paper escaped the notice of both Foreign Affairs and the Cabinet. Foreign Affairs later expressed regret at the oversight (Fergusson 2010, 156).

12. Political candidates talked about Canada as a border risk long after 9/11 and this idea crept into popular culture as well. The US TV series *The West Wing* referred to terrorists "crossing a non-existent Ontario-Vermont border" (Clarkson 2002, 403) and in a feature film in 2006, *The Sentinel*, "a plot to assassinate the president originates in Toronto!" (Thompson and Randall 2008, 334).

13. As described by the RCMP, Integrated Border Enforcement Teams "enhance border integrity and security along the shared Canada/U.S. border, between designated ports of entry, by identifying, investigating and interdicting persons, organizations and goods that threaten the national security of one or both countries or that are involved in organized criminal activity" (RCMP 2009).

Chapter 6

1. Once again, perspectives based on realism, liberalism, the world of ideas, and the government and domestic politics will be brought to bear in order to account for events in Can/Am security relations.

2. Details provided here about that meeting are from the debriefing with media held in the Rose Garden.

3. These and other concerns on the part of the government are presented in Chrétien (2008, 302).

4. Even critics of a military-oriented foreign policy questioned the wisdom of a flat "no" to the US on the subject of BMD. Talks would have the value of protecting NORAD as an invaluable aspect of security cooperation (Welsh 2004, 231).

5. Fergusson (2005a), however, interprets the Bush statement in Halifax as merely expressing hope for cooperation.

6. A source close to the prime minister, however, insists that the subject never came up during decision making (Goldenberg 2006, 297).

7. On 23 March 2005, Canada, the US, and Mexico had launched the Security and Prosperity Partnership during a meeting at Waco, Texas. The short-lived Partnership produced annual summit meetings until its cancellation in August 2009. It would be fair to say that the earlier three-way version focused mostly on economic issues, produced few substantive results, and encountered substantial resistance from both elites and publics until its demise. Canada and the US, in essence, jettisoned Mexico from further discussions of perimeter security.

8. As a side point on the new Canadian assertiveness, note that agreement to help Libya contrasted with refusal to participate in any kind of bailout during the eurozone crisis around the same time. Harper took this position in spite of the fact that the crisis affected numerous NATO allies.

Chapter 7

1. Representative treatments of Canadian foreign policy in its traditional middle-power role are available in James, Michaud, and O'Reilly (2006).

2. The mirror-image problem in the US is a tendency to understate differences. The US is "self-absorbed" and does not think about Canada (Dyment 2010, 35, 34). The humorist Rick Mercer brings this out quite effectively in his television show *Talking to Americans*, which reveals Americans' surprisingly low levels of knowledge about Canada across the board.

3. Fixation on the US, in fact, is likely a throwback to the imperial connection with Britain; see Dyment (2010, 30).

References

Afghanistan Compact. 2006. The London Conference on Afghanistan, London, England, 31 January–1 February.

Arctic Waters Pollution Prevention Act, RSC 1985, c. A-12. Available online.

Baker, Doctor Biff. 2006. "The Final Report of the Canada-United States Bi-National Planning Group." *Canadian Military Journal* 7: 92–95.

Barry, Donald. 2007. "Managing Canada-US Relations in the Post-9/11 Era: Do We Need a Big Idea?" In *Readings in Canadian Foreign Policy: Classic Debates and New Ideas*, edited by Duane Bratt and Christopher J. Kukucha, 116–38. Don Mills, ON: Oxford University Press.

Bercuson, David J. 2005. "The Overview: A New Approach to Canadian Foreign Policy?" In *In the Canadian Interest? Assessing Canada's International Policy Statement*, edited by David J. Bercuson and Denis Stairs, 6–10. Calgary: Canadian Defence & Foreign Affairs Institute.

Bercuson, David J., and Denis Stairs. 2005. "Introduction—Canada's International Policy Statement: What's New, What's Old, and What's Needed." In *In the Canadian Interest? Assessing Canada's International Policy Statement*, edited by David J. Bercuson and Denis Stairs, 1–5. Calgary: Canadian Defence & Foreign Affairs Institute.

Biette, David. 2008. "Resolving Disputes: No One Path." In *Canada and the United States: Differences That Count*. 3rd ed. Edited by David M. Thomas and Barbara Boyle Torrey, 387–403. Peterborough, ON: Broadview Press.

Blatchford, Christie. 2008. *Fifteen Days: Stories of Bravery, Friendship, Life and Death from Inside the New Canadian Army*. Toronto: Anchor Canada.

Bothwell, Robert. 2006. *The Penguin History of Canada*. Toronto: Penguin Canada.

Bow, Brian. 2009. *The Politics of Linkage: Power, Interdependence, and Ideas in Canada-US Relations*. Vancouver: UBC Press.

Brecher, Michael. 1972. *The Foreign Policy System of Israel: Setting, Images, Process*. New Haven, CT: Yale University Press.

Broadhead, Lee-Anne. 2010. "Canadian Sovereignty versus Northern Security: The Case for Updating Our Mental Map of the Arctic." *International Journal* LXV: 913–30.

Burney, Derek. 2005. "Canada-US Relations: Promise Pending?" In *In the Canadian Interest? Assessing Canada's International Policy Statement*, edited by David J. Bercuson and Denis Stairs, 12–17. Calgary: Canadian Defence & Foreign Affairs Institute.

———. 2011. *Libya: Why Are We Involved*. Calgary: Canadian Defence & Foreign Affairs Institute.

Bush, George W. 2010. *Decision Points*. New York: Crown Publishers.

Canada. 2011a. *Canada's Engagement in Afghanistan: Quarterly Report to Parliament for the Period of October 1 to December 31*. Ottawa: Government of Canada.

Canada. Canada's Northern Strategy. 2009a. *Canada's Northern Strategy: Our North, Our Heritage, Our Future*. Government of Canada: Minister of Indian Affairs and Northern Development and Federal Interlocutor for Métis and Non-Status Indians. Available online.

———. 2011b. *Exercising Our Arctic Sovereignty*. Government of Canada. Available online.

Canada. Independent Panel on Canada's Future Role in Afghanistan (Independent Panel). 2008. *Final Report*. Ottawa: Government of Canada.

Canada. Minister of Public Works and Government Services Canada. 2011c. *Canada's State of Trade: Trade and Investment Update 2011*. Ottawa: Government of Canada.

Canada. Office of the Prime Minister. 2006a. "Securing Canadian Sovereignty in the Arctic." Government of Canada, 12 August. Available online.

————. 2007. "Prime Minister Announces Expansion of Canadian Forces Facilities and Operations in the Arctic." Government of Canada, 10 August. Available online.

————. 2008. "PM Announces Government of Canada Will Extend Jurisdiction over Arctic Waters." Government of Canada, 27 August. Available online.

————. 2009b. "PM Announces Construction of New Small Craft Harbour in Pangnirtung." Government of Canada, 20 August. Available online.

————. 2009c. "PM Visits with Canadian Forces Participating in Operation Nanook 09." Government of Canada, 19 August. Available online.

————. 2011d. "Statement by the Prime Minister of Canada While in Paris, France for a Meeting on the Future of Libya." Government of Canada, 1 September. Available online.

————. 2011e. "Statement by the Prime Minister of Canada on the End of NATO-led Libyan mission." Government of Canada, 28 October. Available online.

Canada. Royal Canadian Air Force. 2011f. "Update on Operation Mobile." Government of Canada, 9 June. Available online.

Canada. Standing Committee on National Defence. 2010. *Canada's Arctic Sovereignty*. Ottawa: Government of Canada. Available online.

Canada. Standing Committee on National Security and Peace. 2006b. *Managing Turmoil: The Need to Upgrade Canadian Foreign Aid and Military Strength to Deal with Massive Change*. Ottawa: Government of Canada.

Canada and the United States of America (US). 2011. *United States-Canada Beyond the Border: A Shared Vision for Perimeter Security and Economic Competitiveness—Action Plan*. Ottawa and Washington, DC: Governments of Canada and the United States of America.

Canadian Broadcasting Corporation (CBC). 2006. "Harper Brushes Off U.S. Criticism of Arctic Plan." CBC News, 26 January. Available online.

————. 2011. "Canada to Help Rebuild Libyan Economy, Democracy." CBC News, 22 October. Available online.

Canwest News Service (Canwest). 2008. "U.S. Concerned with New Canadian Shipping Rules in Arctic." Canada.com, 28 August. Available online.

Carnaghan, Matthew, and Allison Goody. 2006. *Canadian Arctic Sovereignty*. Ottawa: Library of Parliament, Parliamentary Information and Research Service.

Center for the Study of the Presidency and Congress (CSPC). 2008. *Afghanistan Study Group Report: Revitalizing Our Efforts, Rethinking Our Strategies*. Washington, DC: CSPC.

Chaplin-Thomas, Charmion. 2011. "CF Helps Canadians and Friends Leave Strife-Torn Libya." National Defence and the Canadian Forces, 28 February. Available online.

Chapnick, Adam. 2002. "Collaborative Independence: Canadian-American Relations in Afghanistan." *International Journal* 57: 341–48.

Chaudhuri, Rudra, and Theo Farrell. 2011. "Campaign Disconnect: Operational Progress and Strategic Obstacles in Afghanistan, 2009–2011." *International Affairs* 87: 271–96.

Choquette-Levy, Nicolas, and Patrick James. 2011. "Structural Realism and Transaction Costs in the U.S.-Canadian Partnership." In *Foreign Partnership Redux: Canada-U.S. Relations in the 21st Century*, edited by Greg Anderson and Christopher Sands, 31–55. Amherst, NY: Cambria Press.

Chrétien, Jean. 2008. *My Years as Prime Minister*. Toronto: Viking Canada.

Clark, Campbell. 2011. "With Libyan Liberation, a Political Victory for Harper." *Globe and Mail*, 20 October. Available online.

Clarkson, Stephen. 2002. *Uncle Sam and Us: Globalization, Neoconservatism, and the Canadian State*. Toronto and Washington, DC: University of Toronto Press and Woodrow Wilson Center Press.

Conservative Party of Canada. 2006. *Stand Up for Canada*. Ottawa: Conservative Party of Canada.

Day, Adam. 2010. *Witness to War: Reporting on Afghanistan 2004–2009*. Kingston, ON: Canadian Defense Academy Press.

defenceWeb. 2011. "Canadian Aircraft Return from Libyan Mission." *defenceWeb*, 4 November. Available online.

Department of Foreign Affairs and International Trade (DFAIT). 2003. *The Canada-U.S. Smart Border Declaration Action Plan for Creating a Secure and Smart Border*. Ottawa: Government of Canada. Available online.

———. 2011a. "Canada Announces Successful Conclusion to Libya Mission." Government of Canada, 28 October. Available online.

———. 2011b. "Canada Extends Its Engagement in Libya." Government of Canada, 26 September. Available online.

———. 2011c. *Canada's Achievements in Afghanistan to Date*. Ottawa: Government of Canada. Available online.

———. 2011d. "Minister Baird Moves to Expel Remaining Libyan Diplomats." Government of Canada, 8 August. Available online.

———. 2011e. "Minister Baird Tables 11th and 12th Quarterly Reports on Canada's Engagement in Afghanistan." Government of Canada, 15 June. Available online.

———. 2011f. "Statement by Minister Baird Updating Canada's Involvement in Libya." Government of Canada, 13 September. Available online.

———. 2011g. *With the Canadian Forces in Afghanistan: Mission Transition and a New Challenge*. Ottawa: Government of Canada. Available online.

Department of National Defence (DND). 2008. *Canada First Defence Strategy*. Ottawa: Government of Canada.

Department of National Defence and the Canadian Forces (DND/CF). 2011. "Take Note Debate: Canadian Forces Involvement in Libya in Support of UNSC Resolution 1973." *DND/CF News*, 21 March. Available online.

Dey, Anouk. 2011. "The Chosen War: How Canada Was Socialized to Fight in Afghanistan." Submitted in partial completion of the degree of M.Phil in International Relations, University of Oxford.

Doran, Charles F. 1984. *Forgotten Partnership: U.S. Canada Relations Today*. Baltimore: Johns Hopkins University Press.

———. 2006. "Canada-U.S. Relations: Personality, Pattern, and Domestic Politics." In *Handbook of Canadian Foreign Policy*, edited by Patrick James, Nelson Michaud, and Marc O'Reilly, 389–408. Lanham, MD: Lexington Books.

Dyment, David. 2010. *Doing the Continental: A New Canadian-American Relationship*. Toronto: Dundurn Press.

Fergusson, James. 2005a. "Shall We Dance: The Missile Defence Decision, NORAD Renewal, and the Future of Canada-U.S. Defence Relations." *Canadian Military Journal* 6 (Summer): 13–22.

———. 2005b. "Canada-United States Defence Relations." In *In the Canadian Interest? Assessing Canada's International Policy Statement*, edited by David J. Bercuson and Denis Stairs, 62–68. Calgary: Canadian Defence & Foreign Affairs Institute.

————. 2010. *Canada and Ballistic Missile Defence, 1954–2009: Déjà Vu All Over Again*. Vancouver: UBC Press.

Fitzsimmons, Dan. 2009. "Transformation in the Canadian Forces: A Sociological Institutionalist Approach to Change in the CF from Peacekeeper to War Fighter." Paper presented to the Canadian Political Science Association, Ottawa, 28 May.

Fletcher, Joseph, Heather Bastedo, and Jennifer Hove. 2009. "Losing Heart: Declining Support and the Political Marketing of the Afghanistan Mission." *Canadian Journal of Political Science* 42: 911–37.

Goldenberg, Eddie. 2006. *The Way It Works: Inside Ottawa*. Toronto: McClelland & Stewart.

Gotlieb, Allan. 2004. *Romanticism and Realism in Canada's Foreign Policy*. Toronto: C.D. Howe Institute.

Graham, William. 2008. *Text of the Canada-US Security Cooperation Agreement*. Ottawa: Government of Canada. Available online.

Granatstein, J.L. 2002. *Canada's Army: Waging War and Keeping the Peace*. Toronto: University of Toronto Press.

————. 2005. "Restructuring for Task Force Deployment." In *In the Canadian Interest? Assessing Canada's International Policy Statement*, edited by David J. Bercuson and Denis Stairs, 74–79. Calgary: Canadian Defence & Foreign Affairs Institute.

Granatstein, J.L., and Dean F. Oliver. 2011. *The Oxford Companion to Canadian Military History*. Don Mills, ON: Oxford University Press.

Hart, Michael. 2008. *From Pride to Influence: Towards a New Canadian Foreign Policy*. Vancouver: UBC Press.

Harvey, Frank. 2007. "The Homeland Security Dilemma: Imagination, Failure and the Escalating Costs of Perfecting Security." *Canadian Journal of Political Science* 40: 283–316.

————. 2011. "The Homeland Security Dilemma: Assessing the Implications for Canada-U.S. Border Security Negotiations." In *Assessing North American Security Relations Ten Years After 9/11*, edited by Jonathan Paquin and Patrick James. Vancouver: UBC Press, forthcoming.

Hawkes, Arthur. 1919. *The Birthright: A Search for the Canadian Canadian and the Larger Loyalty*. Toronto: J.M. Dent & Sons.

Hillier, General Rick. 2010. *A Soldier First: Bullets, Bureaucrats and the Politics of War*. Toronto: HarperCollins Publishers.

Hobson, Sharon Waymont. 2005. "The Defence Policy Statement and Procurement." In *In the Canadian Interest? Assessing Canada's International Policy Statement*, edited by David J. Bercuson and Denis Stairs, 91–96. Calgary: Canadian Defence & Foreign Affairs Institute.

Holland, Kenneth. 2009. *Canadian–United States Engagement in Afghanistan: An Analysis of the "Whole of Government" Approach*. Nova Scotia: The Canadian Peacekeeping Press.

————. 2010. "The Canadian Provincial Reconstruction Team: The Arm of Development in Kandahar Province." *American Review of Canadian Studies* 40: 276–91.

Holland, Kenneth, and Christopher Kirkey. 2010. "Special Issue Introduction: Canada's Commitment to Afghanistan." *American Review of Canadian Studies* 40 (2): 167–70.

Horn, Colonel Bernd. 2010. *No Lack of Courage: Operation Medusa, Afghanistan*. Toronto: Dundurn Press.

Ibbitson, John. 2010. "Harper's Arctic Ice Show: Political Stagecraft Masks Cold Reality." *Globe and Mail*, 25 August. Available online.

International Council on Security and Development. 2011. *Afghanistan Transition and Kabul University: Winning Minds, Losing Hearts*. London, England: ICOS. Available online.

James, Patrick. 2010. *Constitutional Politics in Canada After the Charter: Liberalism, Communitarianism, and Systemism*. Vancouver: UBC Press.

James, Patrick, Nelson Michaud, and Marc O'Reilly. 2006. *Handbook of Canadian Foreign Policy*. Lanham, MD: Lexington Books.

Jockel, Joseph T., and Joel J. Sokolsky. 2008. "Canada and the War in Afghanistan: NATO's Odd Man Out Steps Forward." *Journal of Transatlantic Studies* 6: 100–15.

Kavanagh, Dave. 2005. *S.S. Manhattan & the Northwest Passage*. Sun Ship Historical Society. Available online.

Kirton, John, and Jenilee Guebert. 2007. "Two Solitudes, One War: Public Opinion, National Unity and Canada's War in Afghanistan." Paper presented at Quebec and War conference, University of Montreal, Montreal, QC, 5–6 October.

Kite, Cynthia, and Douglas Nord. 2007. "Canadian Foreign Policy." In *Canadian Studies in the New Millennium*, edited by Patrick James and Mark Kasoff, 245–76. Toronto: University of Toronto Press.

Lackenbauer, P. Whitney, and Matthew Farish. 2007. "The Cold War on Canadian Soil: Militarizing a Northern Environment." *Environmental History* 12: 920–50.

Lajeunesse, Adam. 2007–8. "Sovereignty, Security and the Canadian Nuclear Submarine Program." *Canadian Military Journal* 8: 74–82.

Lasswell, Harold D. 1941. "The Garrison State." *American Journal of Sociology* 46: 455–58.

Lennox, Patrick. 2009. *At Home and Abroad: The Canada-US Relationship and Canada's Place in the World*. Vancouver: UBC Press.

Macdonald, George E.C. 2005. In *In the Canadian Interest? Assessing Canada's International Policy Statement*, edited by David J. Bercuson and Denis Stairs, 55–61. Calgary: Canadian Defence & Foreign Affairs Institute.

Maley, William. 2008. "Provincial Reconstruction Teams in Afghanistan—How They Arrived and Where They Are Going." *NATO Review* 2–4 (IV): 16–19.

"The Manhattan's Epic Voyage." 1969. *Time Magazine*, 26 September. Available online.

Martin, Paul. 2008. *Hell or High Water: My Life In and Out of Politics*. Toronto: McClelland & Stewart.

Massie, Justin. 2013. "Balancing and Bandwagoning in Canada's Evolving Strategic Cultures." In *Assessing North American Security Relations Ten Years After 9/11*, edited by Jonathan Paquin and Patrick James. Vancouver: UBC Press.

Meyer, Carl. 2011. "Extent of Canadian Involvement in Libya Flying Under the Radar." *Embassy*, 6 April. Available online.

Meyer, Karl E. 2003. "Macho America, Diffident Canada." *World Policy Journal* 20: 103–6.

Moore, William Henry. 1918. *The Clash: A Study in Nationalities*. Toronto: J.M. Dent & Sons.

Murray, Melanie. 2011. *For Your Tomorrow: The Way of an Unlikely Soldier*. Toronto: Random House Canada.

NORAD, NORTHCOM, and CANCOM. 2006. *Tri Command Vision*. Ottawa and Washington, DC: Governments of Canada and United States of America.

Nord, Douglas C. 2006. "Canada as a Northern Nation: Finding a Role for the Arctic Council." In *Handbook of Canadian Foreign Policy*, edited by Patrick James, Nelson Michaud, and Marc O'Reilly, 289–315. Lanham, MD: Lexington Books.

———. 2007. "Searching for the North in North American Foreign Policies: Canada and the United States." *American Review of Canadian Studies* 37: 207–17.

Nossal, Kim Richard. 2005. "The Responsibility to Be Honest." In *In the Canadian Interest? Assessing Canada's International Policy Statement*, edited by David J. Bercuson and Denis Stairs, 39–42. Available online.

Owen, Taylor. 2010. "A World Turned Upside Down." *Literary Review of Canada*. Available online.

Paquin, Jonathan, and Louis Bélanger. 2013. "Security Coordination Under the North American Security and Prosperity Partnership, 2005–2009." In *Assessing North American Security Relations Ten Years After 9/11*, edited by Jonathan Paquin and Patrick James. Vancouver: UBC Press.

Parker, Richard D., and Zagros Madjd-Sadjadi. 2010. "Emerging Legal Concerns in the Arctic: Sovereignty, Navigation and Land Claim Disputes." *Polar Record* 46 (239): 336–48.

Payton, Laura. 2011. "John Baird Hints at Libyan Expansion." CBC News, 30 August. Available online.

Pigott, Peter. 2007. *Canada in Afghanistan: The War So Far*. Toronto: Dundurn Press.

Potter, Evan. 2008. "Public Perceptions of Canada-US Relations: Regionalism and Diversity." In *The World in Canada: Diaspora, Demography, and Domestic Politics*, edited by David Carment and David Bercuson, 149–68. Montreal and Kingston: McGill-Queen's University Press.

redOrbit. 2009. "Bush Directive Lays Out US Interest in Arctic." redOrbit.com, 13 January. Available online.

Renuart, Jr., Victor E. 2009. "The Enduring Value of NORAD." *Joint Force Quarterly* 54: 92–96.

Richter, Andrew. 2006. "Forty Years of Neglect, Indifference, and Apathy: The Relentless Decline of Canada's Armed Forces." In *Handbook of Canadian Foreign Policy*, edited by Patrick James, Nelson Michaud, and Marc O'Reilly, 51–82. Lanham, MD: Lexington Books.

Royal Canadian Mounted Police (RCMP). 2009. *Integrated Border Enforcement Teams*. Ottawa: RCMP. Available online.

Sachs, Sue. 2011. "Canadians Complete Final Afghan Operation." *Globe and Mail*, 6 June (updated 7 June). Available online.

Saideman, Stephen M., and David P. Auerswald. 2012. "Comparing Caveats: Understanding the Sources of National Restrictions upon NATO's Mission in Afghanistan." *International Studies Quarterly* 56 (1).

Sands, Christopher. 2011. *America and the Canadian Presence*. Washington, DC: Hudson Institute.

Schiller, Bill. 2006. "The Road to Kandahar." *Toronto Star.* CIGI Online, 8 September. Available online.

Shadwick, Martin. 2006. "The Peacekeeping Blues." *Canadian Military Journal* 8: 94–95.

Sinno, Abdulkader H. 2010. *Organizations at War in Afghanistan and Beyond*. Ithaca, NY: Cornell University Press.

Sjolander, Claire Turenne. 2009. "A Funny Thing Happened on the Road to Kandahar: The Competing Faces of Canadian Internationalism?" *Canadian Foreign Policy* 15: 78–98.

Smith, Gordon. 2007. *Canada in Afghanistan: Is It Working?* Calgary: Canadian Defence & Foreign Affairs Institute.

Sokolsky, Joel J., and Philippe Lagassé. 2006. "Suspenders and a Belt: Perimeter and Border Security in Canada-US Relations." *Canadian Foreign Policy* 12: 15–29.

St. John, Ronald Bruce. 2011. *Libya: Continuity and Change*. London and New York: Routledge.

Stairs, Dennis. 1974. *The Diplomacy of Constraint: Canada, the Korean War and the United States*. Toronto: University of Toronto Press.

Stein, Janice Gross, and Eugene Lang. 2007. *The Unexpected War: Canada in Kandahar*. Toronto: Viking Canada.

Thompson, John Herd, and Stephen J. Randall. 2008. *Canada and the United States: Ambivalent Allies.* 4th ed. Athens and London: The University of Georgia Press.

Travers, Patrick, and Taylor Owen. 2008. "Between Metaphor and Strategy: Canada's Integrated Approach to Peacebuilding in Afghanistan." *International Journal* 63 (3): 685–702.

"US, Canada to Map Unexplored Arctic Seafloor." 2008. *Oil & Gas Journal* 106 (36): 49.

USA. Office of the Press Secretary. 2011. *United States-Canada Beyond the Border: A Shared Vision for Perimeter Security and Economic Competitiveness.* Action Plan, 4 February. Government of the United States. Available online.

Wattie, Chris. 2008. *Contact Charlie: The Canadian Army, the Taliban and the Battle that Saved Afghanistan.* Toronto: Key Porter Books.

Welsh, Jennifer. 2004. *At Home in the World: Canada's Global Vision for the 21st Century.* Toronto: HarperCollins.

Windsor, Lee, David Charters, and Brent Wilson. 2008. *Kandahar Tour: The Turning Point in Canada's Afghan Mission.* Mississauga, ON: John Wiley & Sons Canada.

Index